6 $\frac{00}{00}$ me

LITERATURE AND KNOWLEDGE

LITERATURE

AND

KNOWLEDGE

BY

Dorothy Walsh

WESLEYAN UNIVERSITY PRESS

Middletown, Connecticut

Library of Congress Catalog Card Number: 69-17792
Manufactured in the United States of America
FIRST EDITION

Contents

Acknowledgments

I wish to make grateful acknowledgment to John Dewey's *Art as Experience* and to Susanne Langer's *Feeling and Form*. In particular, I am indebted to Dewey's important distinction between what is just experience and what is singled out as "an experience." I am also indebted to Langer's distinction between actual experience and virtual experience.

I wish to thank the editors of *The Toronto University Quarterly* for permission to use part of an article of mine first published in that journal for Chapter III, and to thank the editors of *The Journal of Philosophy* for permission to use a substantial part of an earlier published paper entitled "Literature and the Categories" for Chapter V.

LITERATURE AND KNOWLEDGE

I

Introductory Remarks

THIS essay is addressed to those students and lovers of literature who are likely to take an interest in a certain theoretical question that can be raised concerning the object of their devotion. The question is this: What kind of knowledge, if any, does literary art afford? To be sure, words other than "knowledge" are often employed with reference to literature, words such as "understanding," "insight," "revelation," "disclosure." In using "knowledge" for the statement of the general question, there is no intent to rule out the propriety of any of these other words; they are all words of cognitive import or suggestion and, as such, may be included in the most general meaning of the term "knowledge."

If works of literary art are in some sense revelatory, the claim that this is so will be of interest only if it can be argued that their being revelatory is bound up with their nature and their success *as* works of literary art. No one will take issue with the noncontroversial assertion that a work of literature might happen to contain some factually reliable information, or that a work of literature, being a cultural product, can, like any other cultural artifact, be considered as datum for inference. But if the only claim worth consideration and debate is one that asserts not a merely extraneous, but an intimate association of litera-

ture with knowledge, then it might seem that our theoretical question is a crucial question, a question that anyone in any way interested in literary art *must* be concerned to answer. But is this assumption warranted? The
importance of theory depends on the level of abstraction
on which you operate, and there is nothing that compels
anyone to ascend to any particular level of abstraction. It
is sometimes difficult for theorists, carried away as they
are, and no doubt should be, by the interest in their theoretical problem or question, to recognize the optional
character of theory, but it is necessary that they do so.

Such a question as: What is poetry? is a theoretical
question. Now if someone, let us say a talented poet, is not
prepared to offer an answer to this question, can we conclude that he does not know what poetry is? It takes only
a little reflection to tell us that we cannot. There is something preposterous in the suggestion that the poet does not
know what poetry is. He knows how to make a poem,
which is not to say that he has a formula, he knows how to
select and revise, he has a developed sense of better and
worse, he recognizes poetry on encounter, he distinguishes
it from other things, and so on. He knows all right, but
this is not to say that he has a theory or that he needs a
theory. To suppose that he needs a theory is to assume that
poetry is created according to theory, and we certainly do
not entertain this view. To be sure, a literary artist may
have a theory, and this theory may be casually efficacious
in energizing his creative activity, but, if so, its value lies
in its energizing power rather than in its cogency as theory. Of course we are interested in what a poet says about
poetry, for this may help us to a better understanding
of his poetry. But in so far as pronouncements approach
the generality of theory, it will be sensible to remember
that the first concern of the literary artist, as artist, is
with his own work, that in so far as artists can be taught
they are taught by the performance of other artists, that

their interest in the work of other artists is largely controlled by the search for stimulating nourishment, and for this reason the interest can be highly selective. Manifestoes, issued by groups of congenial artists, to the effect that only such and such is worth doing, and everything else is mistaken and wrong, can be violently partisan. They are none the worse for that if they are understood not as debatable theories but as proclamations of a direction of interest.

The issue of theory may seem to play a larger role in the more detached and judicious activity of criticism proper. All the same, we can easily overestimate its importance even here. The literary critic cannot afford the degree of partisanship or selective bias that might happen to characterize the artist. The critic must have travelled extensively in the realm of literature, he must have a greater catholicity of taste, a greater interest in and sympathetic understanding of different kinds of literary enterprise. But if we suppose, as surely we should, that practical criticism requires talent, this talent is exhibited in the critic's encounter with the individual work of literature. What he makes of this encounter will depend upon ✓ his perceptive insight and his funded knowledge of other works of literature. To speak of knowledge as funded means that it has been so thoroughly assimilated that it can be used with spontaneity on the relevant occasion. If the practical critic does not have this background of funded knowledge and this capacity to hear the individual voice of the individual work of literature, he lacks what he primarily needs and no theory can possibly supply that need.

There is, of course, theory of criticism which may be distinguished from the enterprise of practical criticism, and the question of whether works of literary art can be said to be revelatory or cognitively significant will come up for consideration here in so far as it may be involved in theory of interpretation and theory of appraisal. Yet theory of criticism is concerned with much more than this particular question of literature and knowledge. What, then, is the interest that might attach to the question? The interest is broadly philosophical; it concerns the role of literary art in human experience, in culture, in civilization.

The primary interest of the student of literature is, naturally and quite appropriately, the interest in exploring the realm of literature which, whatever the uncertainty of its boundaries, presents itself as a country in its own right. This exploration involves not simply the cultivation of acquaintance with individual works of literature but also the recognition of similarities and differences existing between them. All grouping involves some sort of classification, and although classification can be made on the basis of different considerations such as genre, theme, or style, all classification involves an element of abstraction and therefore of theory. Croce's polemical attack on "literary and artistic kinds" is based on the view that any recogniton of a thing as a case of a kind is inimical to its recognition as a distinctive individual entity, but this claim is surely questionable. Are we really prepared to say that we have a better chance of discerning individual style if we know nothing about the common characteristics of period style, that what is distinctive in the literary treatment of a theme is best discerned if we can be happily unaware of any other handling of this theme, that the recognition of *Lycidas* as a pastoral elegy must debar us from any appreciation of it as the poem it is? Of course classification, like everything else, can be abused, and there is, as I shall later argue, a sense in which the good reader must be able to practice a certain innocence in initial reception, but innocence, so understood, is a cultivated spiritual grace and not at all the same thing as simple ignorance.

This exploration *within* the realm of literature will

give rise to comparisons and contrasts, to groupings and orderings, and to the formulation and analysis of literary concepts. But a literary concept is one thing and a concept of literature is something different. To ask: What is literature? is to ask a question of greater theoretical generality than any strictly literary question. To be sure, any attempt to provide an answer must be based on acquaintance with works of literature, but it also requires a contrast of literature with something else. A work of literature, whatever else it may be, is a linguistic composition, but if not every linguistic composition is appropriately considered a work of literature, the question arises as to the basis for distinction, and this requires a transition beyond the realm of literature and an inspection of it from without. Not everyone concerned with literature, no matter how intense his preoccupation, will be interested in pursuing a question of such theoretical generality as the question about literature and knowledge. This is not because questions become more difficult as they become more broadly theoretical, for it is not at all evident that this is so; it is because, for some persons, questions become less interesting as they become more theoretical.

An interest in theory is an interest like any other, and it is important to recognize that if theory is not mandatory neither is it menacing. Theory-suspicion, amounting sometimes to theory-hatred, is based on the mistaken assumption that theory is, or seeks to be, legislative, when in fact it is speculative. Theory is, of course, assertive, and it is desirable, rather than otherwise, that theory should assert its claims in a manner as clear and forthright as can be contrived. This is because theory seeks to recommend itself on the basis of argument, and the relevance and cogency of argument can be assessed only when it is evident what argument is argument for. Since theory, by its very nature, is speculative, argumentative and controversial, the proper attitude towards theory is never willing suspension of disbelief but always critical scrutiny. Proffered answers to questions can be of interest only to those who ask these questions, or to those who find that they take an interest in these questions when they are raised. But to enjoy theory the interest aroused by a theoretical question must be something more lively than a mere willingness to hear and to consider what someone has to offer in the way of an answer. The interest should be such that any nonacceptance leads to the self-directed question: If I do not think this, then what do I think? Theory is not only the result of reflection, it should be provocative of reflection. In short, a theoretical question should show like the golden hind that starts from the thicket, and one must wish to pursue this quarry.

A possible first response to the question about literature and knowledge might be: "Well, it all depends on what you mean by 'literature' and what you mean by 'knowledge.'" Certainly it does. We all know that the word "literature" can be used in a broad sense so that "the literature on the subject" means "the written discourse on the subject." Thus we may hear reference to "the literature of jurisprudence" or "the literature of philology." Presumably no one is likely to entertain doubts about whether literature in this sense is concerned with knowledge. But "literature" can be given a more restricted meaning, and we have this in mind when we speak of imaginative literature or literary art, or when we say: "By 'literature' I refer to such productions as poems, novels, plays." Such remarks can serve as a rough indication of the object of our inquiry, but it is only a rough indication. We all know, at least on the basis of a little reflection, that persons who are quite evidently using the word "literature" in this more restricted sense can still ask: "What is literature?" or "What is literary art?"

Now we have to face the fact that any attempt to offer

a full answer to this question consists in the elaboration and recommendation of a theory about literature. This being so, we have to face the further fact that it is very unlikely that any such theory will leave open and undecided the issue of literature and knowledge. What, then, do we do? The only thing we can do is to close in on the matter gradually, accepting as point of departure the rough distinction and saying that by "literature" we mean such works as poems, novels, plays.

We face comparable difficulties with respect to the word "knowledge." Though our initial indication of meaning for "literature" allows us to say that a poem or novel is the kind of thing we have in mind, we cannot suppose that our question about literature and knowledge is a straightforward empirical question of the sort that might be met by the injunction: Look and see! It is sensible enough to look into a rock formation to see if we can find gold; we cannot, in the same way, look into a novel or poem to see if we can find knowledge. What may appropriately be called knowledge is controversial in a sense in which what may be called gold is not.

In my initial statement of the question, I said that words other than "knowledge" are frequently used with reference to literature, words such as "understanding," "insight," "disclosure," "revelation," and I went on to assure the reader that, in using the word "knowledge" for the statement of the question, I did not intend to rule out the propriety of any of these other words. This is a promise that is seriously intended and must be kept.

Many modern philosophers of neopositivistic tendency have quite precise convictions on the issue of what may properly be called knowledge and on the permissible or, as they would prefer to say, intelligible meanings of the word "know." These philosophers are likely to experience what might be called "shudders of distaste" in reading the discourse of any literary critic or theorist who, in writing about works of literature, uses such expressions as "revelatory insight" or "illumination." Such philosophers are more than likely to think: "This is the kind of language that calls aloud for philosophical tidying up." But is there not an implicit assumption involved in such a view? And might not this assumption, if stated bluntly and brutally, be productive of raised eyebrows? Consider the following: "This language of the literary critic or theorist needs re-expression. After all, who is this fellow? He's just a devotee of literature and can't then be expected to have any sensitive appreciation of the exact meaning of words."

Now, to be sure, a philosopher, intent on reformulation, might protest that he is concerned only with some linguistic expressions; he might say: "Words such as 'knowledge' and 'truth' have been subjected to long and careful consideration by philosophers, and it can't really be claimed that literary critics and theorists have given the same attention to *these* words." This is so and must be acknowledged. Nevertheless, we have to take account of the fact that philosophers engaged in linguistic analysis are not engaged in improving the Oxford English Dictionary by seeking out subtle nuances of meaning there overlooked. Philosophers are intent on theories, and, since theory of knowledge plays a large role in philsophical discourse, any pronouncement by a philosopher to the effect that such and such is what we mean, or ought to mean, when we speak of knowledge, is a pronouncement associated with a theory.

It is proper for me to say at once that I hold the view that what many contemporary philosophers consider to be permissible meanings of the expression "to know" are too narrow. In the course of this essay I shall offer an argument designed to show that there is a use of "know" that is not uncommon in ordinary talk, and that is accepted as intelligible by persons not predisposed to disallow it because of adherence to some particular theory of knowledge. This is the use of "know" involved when, in reference to some sort of experience, someone says: "You don't really know what it is unless you've undergone it, unless you've lived through it." This way of talk suggests that first-hand "knowing by living through" is not reducible to second-hand "knowing about." I think that this is the case, and that this is a matter that deserves careful attention.

I would not wish to claim that all students and lovers of literature tend naturally to the view that works of literary art, when functioning successfully as such, have some intimate engagement with what may be called knowledge, but I think that many do. I also think that those who do are likely to voice their assumption by using such expressions as "revelatory insight," "heightened understanding," "illumination," "realization," "epiphany." These words do not evoke any shudders of distaste in me because I believe that what lies behind the choice of such words is not muddlement of mind, but, rather, a sense that words such as these more accurately express the kind of cognitive significance works of literature can have. Though I believe that we need a clearer understanding of just what assumptions are involved in the choice and use of such expressions as "revelatory insight," and although, as a theorist, I shall boldly attempt to offer this clarification, I shall seek to do this in such a way as not to disallow these words but, rather, to conserve them.

The remarks I have so far offered will clearly suggest to the reader that my answer to the question: Do works of literary art, when functioning successfully as such, have any intimate engagement with what may be called knowledge? Is Yes. Indeed it is the purpose of this essay to offer a reasoned defense of this affirmative answer. As I said before, I do not take it for granted that all lovers and students of literature will naturally tend to assume that an affirmative answer is a proper answer. There are, I believe, those who will be inclined to think that an affirmative answer is, and must be, based on a disregard of the status of literature as art. Their point of view could be roughly expressed as follows: "Works of literary art have too often been treated as if they were some form of straightforward discourse about this and that. But the view of literature as 'discourse about' is mistaken, and cannot be justified on the basis of the mere consideration that literature is linguistic. Art is essentially creation. A created work of art is an autonomous structure; it is not about anything, it is just itself. Surely in this day and age it is high time that those who deal with literature should recognize that they are dealing with art."

Now, as to this, I shall say at once that I agree that a work of literary art is not suitably regarded as a straightforward discourse about something, and called "literature" merely because it can be seen to have some elegance in mode of expression. In seeking to offer a meaning for "literature" which, though not complete, is more precise than the initial statement: "By 'literature' I refer to such things as poems, novels, plays," I shall offer an account designed to emphasize what literary art has in common with the other arts. But I hold the view that it is quite possible to recognize a general affinity between the arts without supposing that they are so alike that if the issue of knowledge is not relevant to decorative design, or architecture, or music, it follows that it cannot be relevant to literary art. If it is general pattern of compositional design that makes literature art, it is language that makes it literature. Accordingly, we may ask: Can something be created by language organized as art that cannot be created by line and color or by musical tone so organized? If the answer to this is yes, as I believe it is, the recognition of literature as art does not necessarily preclude the further recognition that talk about revelatory insight may, after all, be quite sensible in reference to *this* art. In short, literary art can be no less art for being a distinctive art with special pecularities of its own.

In the light of all these remarks, it should be evident to the reader that although my final answer to the question about literature and knowledge is yes, any defense of this answer will necessarily involve a theory about literature, and also a marking out and reasoned justification of the particular meaning to be ascribed to "knowledge" in this connection. Otherwise expressed, the conclusion to which I hope to move will have to be of the form: Literature (considered to be such and such) can properly be said to have some intimate engagement with knowledge (considered to be such and such). This being so, it follows that if we have to close in gradually on a meaning for "literature" we also have to close in gradually on a meaning for "knowledge." I realize very well that this procedure of closing in gradually can be irritating to those who wish to have questions formulated with high precision in initial presentation. I confess that I too like to have this initial precision when it can be supplied without prejudgment of the issues involved. But when we are faced with a question that involves two terms, the meaning of each of which is controversial, the only way the question can be made precise is by an act of decision on the issue of meaning, and any such act of decision will be more than likely to prejudice the answer.

Still, someone may protest: "That's all very well, but surely if we know anything we know that nothing but confusion and waste of time is likely to result when persons launch into discussion without any clear notion of what they are talking about." True. But what I call "closing in gradually" need not involve this disastrous and disabling vagueness. For example, one question which I shall discuss in the course of this essay may be stated as follows: Can we find in works of literary art, such as poems or novels, some sort of explicit or implicit claim about man, or the world, or the human condition? If we can, does the value of a work of literature depend in whole, or in part, on the truth or warrantability of this claim? Now here we have a question that is reasonably precise in formulation and also a question that, in any discussion of the general topic of literature and knowledge, ought to come up for consideration. However, I hold the view that although this is *a* question that can and should be raised, it is not *the* question in the sense of the only question. Considering the issue of literature and knowledge from the point of view of this question is one way of considering it. There are others. Thus what I call closing in gradually on the issue does not mean that I hope to evade, or think it proper to evade, the task of formulating questions. All it means is that we should not, from the very beginning, prejudge the answer by supposing that there is one and only one point of view from which the topic can be considered

The question about literature and knowledge is an old question, and although I do not propose to offer a history of opinion on the subject, it will be useful to begin with a consideration of Plato's troubled reflection concerning the poets. It would be a mistake to suppose that Plato just disliked poetry. He fully concedes the greatness, as well as the charm, of Homer, and tells us that the renunciation of poetry will "cost a struggle." But why should we be asked to suffer this struggle and to submit to this renunciation? To understand what is involved requires an act of historical imagination.

Today it would not occur to any of us to suppose that the kind of writing engaged in by poets, and other literary artists, constitutes a threat to those whose interest lies in the nonliterary treatment of subject matter. If a poet speaks of the moon as a goddess, no astronomer supposes that he must do battle against this mode of talk before he can win recognition for a scientific discourse on the moon.

Yet this was not always so. Early attempts at explanation of why things are as they are, and why events happen as they do, tended to be in the form of mythic stories. So long as such stories were taken as adequate and sufficient accounts, their acceptance constituted an impediment to any other and different mode of explanation. Plato remarks that there is "an old quarrel between philosophy and poetry." Philosophy, in this context, must be taken to include any kind of discourse that seeks to establish its claims by reasoning and by argument. But how can sober rational discourse make its way against the eloquence of poets? Poets are charmers, poets are verbal magicians.

Yet if this "old quarrel" based on rivalry has now been mediated by the device of disengagement, so that literary art is one thing, and nonliterary discourse something else, we still need to consider the implications of this disengagement. Roughly stated, there are two views that might be taken. According to one view, the separation can be seen as the liberation of literature from the alien and extraneous burden of cognitive concern. So liberated, literature is free to develop its potentialities strictly as art. According to the other view, the disengagement provides the opportunity for the recognition of the distinctive kind of cognitive significance literary art can have.

Before launching upon a more detailed examination of the theme of literature and knowledge, let us consider briefly the troubled reflection of Plato on the topic of poets.

II

Plato's Problem

"And we might also allow her [poetry's] champions, who
are not poets, but lovers of poetry, to publish a prose de-
fence on her behalf, showing that she is not only pleasant
but also useful for political constitutions and for human
life, and we shall listen with friendly feelings. For it will
be to our profit if she is made out to be not only pleasant,
but useful."

"Most certainly to our profit," he said.

"But if not, my dear comrade, then, as men who have
loved but who have come to the conclusion that their love
is unprofitable, though it may cost a struggle yet turn
away; so likewise, though by reason of the love for such
poetry as our nurture in beautiful constitutions has bred
in us we shall be glad of any manifestation of her goodness
and truth yet until she is able to defend herself, we will
not listen to her without repeating to ourselves as a charm
this argument of ours and this incantation, for fear of fall-
ing again into that childish love which is still shared by the
many. We shall chant, therefore, that this poetry is not to
be taken seriously, as though it were a solemn performance
that had to do with truth, but that he who hears it is to
keep watch on it, fearful for the city in his soul, and that
we may lay down these laws concerning poetry which we
have described." (Trans: A. D. Lindsay)

It is thus, in the tenth book of the *Republic,* that the Platonic Socrates concludes his indictment of poetry, and this is the charge to which various counsels for the defense, from Aristotle through Sidney to Shelley and beyond, have addressed themselves. Yet the question can be raised as to whether this defense is at all necessary. Why should poetry have to be defended as useful and true? Could not the end of poetry be simply delight, and is not delight a self-sufficient good? If so, then, whatever confusion of mind or failure of sensibility trapped Plato into raising irrelevant issues, it will be both tactful and sensible to pass silently over this ancient scandal.

It is not difficult to understand why someone, scrutinizing familiar "briefs for the defense," beginning with Aristotle's *Poetics,* might conclude that poetry is badly served by her self-appointed champions, and that this is a sorry, if inevitable, consequence of accepting the task of defense on lines laid down by Socrates. But no amount of impatience with theorists who would tell us that it is permissible for poets to feign many a thing and to invent what never happened—because by this means poetry can exemplify general truths, such as "How a man of a certain sort would act in a situation of a certain sort," or render moral principles vivid and persuasive by concrete examples—will of itself suffice to establish the view that imaginative literature has nothing to do with knowledge and that there is no meaning of "truth" that has relevance to literary expression.

It is necessary, I think, to try to understand Plato's problem, for though Plato can be wrong he is never just simpleminded, and the issue of poetry engaged him deeply. Taking the dialogues as a whole, we can notice that Socrates speaks of poets and poetry in many voices, sometimes with ironic, provocative detachment, sometimes with bitter antagonism, on occasion in a voice troubled by sudden doubt suggesting the fear of sacrilege and the need for recantation. If, on the whole, Plato is prepared to take a stand against poetry, this is a stand not easily taken, for there is distress, and there is also something of hesitation, in this renunciation.

We may take it that Plato will not be impressed by attempts to show that poets are, after all, innocent, useful, respectable teachers. In an age when the text of Homer was the staple of Greek education, the notion of the poet as teacher was perfectly familiar. But it is the acceptance of the poet as teacher that alarms Plato. There isn't, in Plato's opinion, the slightest doubt that *this* teacher will be persuasive. Poets are verbal magicians, they can charm the birds out of the trees, they can charm you into believing anything, such is the hypnotic power of poetry. Oh this is dangerous! This is why we must mount guard, fearful for the city of the soul. It is so easy to yield to the charm of poetry; you can be conquered before you know what has happened to you. Poetry does not come with argument but with eloquence. Remember, and tell yourself again and again that eloquence is one thing and truth is another.

There are those who will be prompt to say that Plato's anxiety is gratuitous. This anxiety springs from the mistaken view that poetry is in some way assertive, that it can influence belief and that it can deceive. But, "the poet he nothing affirms, and therefore never lyeth." To be sure, all Sidney meant, as can be discovered by putting this quotation back in its context, is that the poet is entitled to invention; we do not have to suppose that animals think and speak as Aesop represents them as doing. The poet is "not labouring to tell you what is or is not, but what should or should not be." So there is, after all, affirmation, and Plato would certainly consider that mounting guard against claim of this sort was much more important than running the risk of factual misinformation on the habits of animals. The notion that a poem, or some other work of literature, is totally without claim of any sort would not have occurred to Plato and for the very good reason that he had only to look about him to observe the suasive influency of poetry.

The tone of voice in which Socrates refers to "this pleasure producing poetry" may suggest a distrust of pleasure simply as such, but though Plato can sound a note of ascetic austerity, as for example in the *Phaedo,* the value of innocent pleasure is fully recognized in the *Philebus.* Plato wants some assurance that a pleasure sought is an innocent pleasure and this, after all, is not such a strange requirement. Thus, if Plato is in error, it will not be because he condemns poetry because it is pleasant, but because he fails to recognize that this pleasure could never be anything other than innocent.

Nor can it be said that Plato is an enemy of beauty. Plato's conception of the beautiful is, on the whole, the classical formalistic conception. Beauty is unity in variety. More fully stated, a beautiful structure is one in which the various parts cooperate harmoniously for the production of the whole, and which is such that the various parts, instead of being curtailed, are, on the contrary, enhanced by their membership in the whole. This formalistic concept of the beautiful admits of application beyond the sphere of the sensuous, and Socrates does not hesitate with his provocative remark that perhaps mathematicians know more about beauty than poets. Still, this is not to deny that poetry might be beautiful. Anything that has structure might have the kind of structure we recognize as beautiful. Whatever we may think of Plato's political philosophy, however much many of us would quickly and unhesitatingly decline invitation to citizenship in the ideal Republic, it remains the case that Plato believed that this political constitution was a beautiful structure—a solution of "the high problem of the One and the Many" in the sphere of politics. We know from the *Symposium* that

Plato held that the recognition of beauty in one sphere prepares us for its recognition in another, and this is the point of the remark that, by reason of the love of such poetry as our nurture in beautiful constitutions has bred in us, we shall be glad to see poetry vindicated if this is possible. Thus poetry, at least some poetry, can be beautiful.

So poetry can be pleasing, indeed alluring, and poetry can be beautiful. Homer, Socrates tells us, is a very great poet; Socrates even wonders whether it is possible to be a better poet than Homer. It will not be easy to give up poetry. We should take quite seriously the remark that this renunciation will cost a struggle. There is every reason to suppose that the renunciation was hard and difficult for Plato, and this not simply because Plato's initial ambition was to be a poet, an ambition he abandoned as a result of his association with Socrates.

There was, of course, an historical Socrates about whom we have some biographical information. Since we cannot simply identify this Socrates with the Socrates met with in the Platonic dialogues, it is tempting to try to build up an idea of him by reference to other sources. Aristotle, in his brief review of the history of philosophy, attributes to the historical Socrates the search for definitions and a moral concern. With reference to the latter, Aristotle also attributes to Sorcates the doctrine commonly known as "the Socratic paradox," though evidently to Socrates himself it was no paradox at all. The argument for this runs as follows: Every man pursues what he takes to be good, why else would he pursue it? If, then, what he seeks or does is not good, he has made an error of judgment. Accordingly, virtue is knowledge, and moral evil has its root in intellectual confusion. Aristotle held that this was paradoxical, meaning not plausible, for it takes no account of the familiar matter of weakness of will and failure of self-control. Now if the historical Socrates professed to find this notion of weakness of will puzzling, or perhaps did find it puzzling, we can understand the extraordinary impact of the personality of Socrates and the legends that grew up about him. The influence of the historical Socrates seems to have been the influence of a personality rather than the influence of any set of doctrines taught, if indeed Socrates can be described as teaching anything.

Socrates astonished, fascinated and exasperated his fellow Athenians. He seems to have been, as nearly as possible, the completely rational man. What is reasonable to believe is what the evidence warrants; what is reasonable to do is what is conducive to the highest good. How could this be otherwise? Furthermore, how could you not believe and act according to the dictates of reason; are you not, after all, a rational being? There is a certain simplicity about a character and personality of this sort. Socrates was all of a piece, and his rock-like independence was associated with this. Many an Athenian must have wondered: Is the fellow human? Legends accumulated about Socrates, legends suggesting that Socrates exercised a self-control not characteristic of other men. Socrates was content with the minimum of worldly goods, yet he did not practice asceticism as a consciously chosen discipline, for Socrates needed no discipline. If invited to a banquet, he was happy to avail himself of the banquet. At the banquet he could drink more wine than anyone else, but he was never drunk. Neither indulgence nor privation could cloud Socrates' mind, and, of course, Socrates could never be intimidated.

If this is the historical Socrates, and there are some grounds for thinking that it is, we cannot suppose that this Socrates could ever have been alarmed by poets. We cannot imagine him "mounting guard fearful for the city of the soul," or devising a chant, an incantation, a counter-magic to offset the magic of the poets. Faced with a poetic utterance, Socrates would quite simply have examined it for its factual accuracy or its logical cogency and accepted or rejected it accordingly. We meet this Socrates from time to time in the Platonic dialogues. For example in *Euthyphro* we have the following:

> Soc. The poet [Stasinus] sings—
> "Of Zeus, the author and creator of all things,
> You will not tell; for where there is fear there is also reverence."
> Now I disagree with this poet. Shall I tell you in what respect?
> EUTH. By all means.
> Soc. I should not say that where there is fear there is also reverence; for I am sure that many persons fear poverty and disease, and the like evils, but I do not perceive that they reverence the objects of their fear.

Thus the statement is inexact and the poet is wrong. Our quick response may be to feel that Socrates is wrong in offering this utterance such a show of critical scrutiny. We might say: Socrates, it is useless to consider the meaning of isolated quotations, poetic utterances have meaning only in the total context of poems. But Socrates would then be likely to ask how it is that poems as a whole can have meaning if parts of poems have no meaning. We might say that though poems and even parts of poems have meaning, yet a poet never asserts anything. But Socrates will then want to know why, if this is so, poets use the indicative language of assertion. The point I wish to bring out here is that if, as is possible, the historical Socrates adopted this forthright procedure of taking poets at their word and holding them to their words, this procedure, backed as it was by the impressive and forceful personality of Socrates, might well have had its effect on the young Plato. Having heard the voice of Socratic reason, how could one forget it?

Regardless of whether this conjecture about the historical Socrates is correct, we can still find *a* Socrates in the Platonic dialogues who answers to this description, a Socrates who is, as it were, the embodiment of the voice of reason. Scrutinizing the grounds for the judgment of banishment of poets, as these grounds are set forth in *Republic X,* we derive the impression that these grounds are two and separate. There is the claim that poetry is dangerous because it can be cognitively persuasive without being cognitively reliable, and there is the claim that poetry is dangerous because it "waters the emotions and makes them grow when these passions should be dried up." The impression of two rather different grounds for objection can be further enforced by a consideration of Aristotle's *Poetics,* for Aristotle's claim that poetry can exhibit or exemplify general truths is one thing, and his claim that poetry, tragedy at any rate, can provide catharsis, a purging of excess passion, is another. However, if we look carefully at what Plato says about the theatre, and the effect of theatrical performance on the spectator, we shall find a connection between the objection on cognitive grounds and the objection on emotive grounds.

Plato is not among those who believe that the question of why tragedy pleases is a difficult question. For Plato there is no puzzle. Consider the themes of tragedy—murder, adultery, matricide, incest, and so on. Horrors, yes, but are you really surprised to discover that people have an appetite for horrors? Is there no fascination in the dark underground of the soul? And there is more to consider. Tragedy administers to the complaining element in us. How we long to complain, to lament our condition, to indulge in self-pity! Under cover of identification with the tragic hero we can gratify our propensity for lamentation. Plato believed that it should be part of the code of a civilized man to keep his desperation quiet. Such a man, whatever his loss, would be ashamed to lament publicly, but in the theatre the spectator loses all sense of individual responsibility. Comedy, in its fashion, is as weakening as tragedy. A man would be ashamed to make the jests he accepts with delight when these are presented on the comic stage. There is an element in us which desires to make these broad jests, and we are easily persuaded that we can enjoy them with impunity when they are made for us by the comic poet. Plato will not be likely to accept a doctrine of catharsis as a kind of mental therapy, a salutary periodic release, for Plato believed that we learn what we practice and that every relaxation of control weakens us.

In the *Phaedrus* the tripartite division of the soul is symbolized by a charioteer and two horses. The charioteer is reason. The beautiful white horse with the straight nose is the embodiment of the noble passions, such as courage and generosity. The tendency of the white horse is always upward, so that this horse would continue upward even if the charioteer relaxed his hold on the reins. But the other horse, the wild black uncouth beast with the bloodshot eyes, is another matter. The tendency of this horse is downward. Moreover, this horse is crafty, cunning, and ever watchful for any slackening of the reins. If the charioteer should be forgetful and let the reins fall slack, this black horse will get the bit in his teeth and plunge downward, dragging the white horse with him, for he is stronger. It takes the combined strength of the charioteer and the white horse to control the black horse. Once the black horse has got his head it will be hard to pull him in. It is a slow and difficult process to curb a runaway horse, to force him to a standstill and turn his head in the opposite direction.

The dramatic poets know to a nicety what will attract us. The trouble is not that they are poor poets, defective dramatists, for they have talent in abundance. The trouble is really the trouble with the theatre. We might request the dramatist to present the rational man, but the sad truth of the matter is that the rational man is not very promising dramatic material.

If we are right in the assumption that the historical Socrates would appear to Plato as the ideal of the rational man, Plato would see in Socrates the living proof of the possibility of the triumph of reason over all the dark forces of the irrational, and the fact that in the historical Socrates this victory is achieved without a struggle—quite simply and naturally—would make it all the more impressive. Socrates turned to reason as naturally as the flower to the light, and it is not difficult to understand the enormous appeal of the totally integrated, and therefore simple, personality for someone as many-faceted and complex as Plato. Plato could feel the charm of poetry and the lure of the irrational, and Plato, though convinced by the rationality of Socrates, could have moments of misgiving. Plato, it is said, was an initiate of the Eleusinian mysteries, and there was an ancient tradition of poetry as divine inspiration.

In the dialogue of the *Ion* we hear a voice that may have been fairly close to the voice of the historical Socrates. Ion is a rhapsode, a reciter of poetry, but Ion, though a skilled rhapsode, is unable to answer satisfactorily any of the questions Socrates puts to him about his art. Socrates plays with him but offers him "a way out." After all, why should Ion be expected to know; he is the vehicle of a divine inspiration, he is possessed. Ion avails himself of this solution, oblivious to the Socratic irony, the effect of which is to suggest: Let us not expect any sense from this fellow; by his own admission he is mad. But the doctrine of divine inspiration receives a different treatment in the *Phaedrus*: a Socrates, who is now more Platonic, makes a distinction between a lower and a higher madness. This higher madness is the madness of love, of prophecy, of the purification rites of the mysteries, and of poetry. The suggestion is strong that to deny the claims of this higher madness is to commit sacrilege. The irrational is, then, not so easily dismissed. There is also a curious incident recounted in the *Phaedo*. When Socrates' friends come to visit him in prison for the last time, Cebes asks why Socrates, who never before wrote a line of poetry, has recently been engaged in turning some of Aesop's fables into verse. Socrates explains that he has had a dream in which he was commanded "to cultivate and make music," so, to satisfy a scruple, he has composed some verses. All this is passed off briefly and lightly, but one can wonder whether this scruple is not Plato's scruple. If Plato's hero, Socrates, has, by any chance, been guilty of something verging on sacrilege, this offense will be expiated before he dies.

But sudden scruple is not all; there is a deeper problem of ambiguity in Plato's position. The counter-magical chant that "this poetry is not to be taken seriously as though it were a solemn performance that had to do with truth" cannot be understood as the statement of a theory —a theory to the effect that the issue of truth should never be raised in connection with poetry. The chant is a warning—a warning to the effect that poetic charm is no guarantee of truth. It is worth noticing that there is one kind of poetry that could be allowed in the ideal republic, "hymns of praise to the gods and famous men." Lyrical expression of laudation would not have the complicated character of epic or dramatic poetry. There would be no point in this exception if, with regard to *all* poetry, Plato was really prepared to take the charm and let the claim to knowledge go. But if we can have the charm without the truth, surely we should be able to have the truth without the charm. If it be acknowledged that allegory and myth, as employed by Plato, are essentially literary devices, we are entitled to ask, and with a certain bluntness, why he needs these devices. It is all very well for Plato to assure us that he believes that what the myth presents is true or "close to the truth," why cannot we have the truth direct? Plato would be in real theoretical trouble if he should be forced to admit that there is a kind of knowledge or insight that can be conveyed by literary means only.

It is difficult to suppose that the use of allegory and myth is a mere device of popular presentation, that is, the finding of an alluring garment in which to clothe, for the benefit of the uninitiated, a doctrine that could be accepted nude by the initiated. It is certainly the case that some of Plato's later compositions, such as *Parmenides* and the *Sophist,* must have been intended for a specialized audience, but this is not a matter of "the same view" differently presented, but of a shift of interest to more technical problems. Even if we say that the doctrine of the Ideas, in its earlier "two-world" version, lent itself more readily to literary expression, we still have to ask why this was so. Certainly there is a difference between reading a story about the ascent of the soul, or the escape from the cave, and reading an argumentative discussion on the logical problems of class inclusion and class exclusion, but this difference cannot be understood as a simple matter of wrong and right views; it is a difference in procedure, in method, in orientation. There is, Socrates tells us, "an old quarrel between philosophy and poetry." Perhaps this is a quarrel that Plato experienced in his own person.

Let us try to understand this quarrel between philosophy and poetry by looking back to the beginning of things. Not really the beginning of things; we cannot look back to that, for we have no way of knowing or even of surmising when men began to devise and recount stories. The only thing we can be sure of is that early story would serve many purposes, and would not be thought of as something distinctive, called "literature" or "literary art." Story, no doubt from initial inception, had its alluring entertainment value. Our remote ancestors, like our little descendants, would gladly be "told a story." But story, in so far as it dealt with the deeds of heroes, would be commemorative and fulfill some of the tasks now assigned to history. Story would also be explanation. The activity of gods served to give an intelligible account of why things are as they are and why events happen as they do. Story was everything. Briefly put, the poets were first on the scene, and every kind of nonliterary discourse had to fight for recognition against the allurement of what might be called the Poetic Establishment.

The dawn of philosophy was, as nearly as anything can be, "a new thing in the world." Thales, citizen of Miletus in the sixth century B.C., is reported to have suggested that the multiplicity of the things in nature is derived from a basic world substance that is of the nature of water. How very odd to say that everything is made out of water! Surely the story of a mystical marriage between an earth goddess and a sky god is ever so much more intelligible as an account of generation! In a way, yes. But all the same, Thales with his queer suggestion is the father of speculative science and of western philosophy. The point, of course, is that Thales' suggestion is open to a kind of critical scrutiny that cannot be easily, if at all, directed to the consideration of a mystical marriage of divinities. Thales' suggestion was not only open to question, it was at once questioned by his fellow citizen and disciple, Anaximander. Pre-Socratic philosophy presents a bewildering display of multiple suggestions. It is as if speculative thought, suddenly released, uncovered possibility after possibility. Philosophy is, from the beginning, characteristically argumentative and contentious, and the recurrent question is: Well, what is the argument?

The reception accorded philosophers was various. The legend that Thales, observing the stars, fell into a well, something that any sensible handmaiden would have had

the wit to avoid, suggests an amused tolerance. But philosophers were often regarded with suspicion. Anaxag-
oras was charged with impiety and Pericles had to see to
his safe removal from Athens. The highly conservative
Aristophanes makes merry at the expense of philosophers. Because Heraclitus had said that a dry soul (a
rational, disintoxicated soul) was the wisest and the best,
Socrates is represented as sitting in a high basket so as to
keep as dry as possible. The satiric intent of the cry "Long
live King Vortex who hath dethroned Zeus!" contrasts the
sound sense of traditional explanations with the contentious nonsense of philosophers. Zeus we can understand,
but vortex, how do we make sense of that?

The quarrel between philosophy and poetry, already
operative before the advent of Socrates, and therefore describable as "old," was a quarrel not over doctrine but
over method. There was plenty of disagreement in doctrine among the philosophers, but for all that they were
united in their very disputation, united in their appeal to
reason and in their common employment of the weapon
of argument. This is the point of the contrast drawn by
Plato between dialectic and rhetoric, argument and eloquence. Both argument and eloquence can be persuasive
but the urgent question was: How can sober, responsible,
rational discourse make its way against the honeyed
voices of the practitioners of poetic magic?

It takes an effort of the historical imagination to understand with appropriate sympathy the position of those pio-
neers who fought the battle for the recognition of nonliterary discourse, for this battle has long since been won. The
"old quarrel" has been resolved, not by the destruction
of either contestant, but by disengagement. Yet the recognition of the fact and the propriety of disengagement does
not insure agreement on what this disengagement means
for theory about literature. Shall we see the disengagement as the liberation of literary art from tasks the per-

formance of which was always extraneous to its essential nature? Shall we see the disengagement as the liberation of Ariel? Ariel was always lovely and gracious even when obliged to run messages and perform other useful tasks, but Ariel is now released from the mundane concern with cognition. Merrily, merrily, shall he live now, and all lovers of literature with him. Or, to the contrary, shall we say that the magic island, which is the domain of literature, cannot be abandoned and that the control of Prospero over both Ariel and Caliban must be sustained, that this magic always had its revelatory illuminating power, and that the disengagement of literary from nonliterary discourse does not tell us that literature has nothing to do with knowledge, but helps us to recognize the distinctive kind of knowledge and manner of knowing peculiar to literature?

This issue cannot be debated without raising the question: What is literature? One cannot assess the cogency of any claim about literature without understanding what the claimant means by "literature." For any theoretical claim, whether this be about literature or anything else, there is always the distinction between the object of discourse and the claim made about it. This means, of course, that the question of relevance is one thing, and the question of cogency another. The issue of relevance is logically prior to the issue of cogency, for the reason that unless relevance is recognized the question of cogency does not arise. But can one offer an account of literature that does not prejudice (prejudge) the issue of literature and knowledge? One can, I think, offer a preliminary account that is not decisive on this matter, provided this account puts aside, for the time being, all consideration of outlying causes and probable effects, and concentrates directly on the examination of structure.

III

What Is Literature?

AS we know, the word "literature" can be used in a broader or in a narrower sense. What is referred to as "the literature of the subject" might be discourse on Roman coinage or on feudal customs; it might be philosophical or legal theory. "The enclosed literature" might be printed instructions on how to assemble some object or on how to use it effectively. In short, "literature" can be any kind of linguistic composition. The question of whether literature can be a source of knowledge is not an interesting question if this is what we mean by "literature." The question has interest only as it refers to literature in the restricted sense and it seems that we can single out this restricted sense if we say that by "literature" we mean literary art. But what is literary art?

Well, we know. But then, again, we can be rather easily assailed by the impression of uncertainty. We know in the sense that we could, without hesitation, provide examples. Virgil's *Aeneid* and Shakespeare's *The Tempest* are, we confidently say, cases of literary art. But we might be troubled if we were asked to explain what it is that makes them such, and we shall certainly be troubled by the recognition that an ability to mention examples by no means insures a capacity for ready decision about *any* linguistic composition. Is it or is it not a case of literary art?

One of the difficulties here is that "art" is not a purely descriptive term; it is not like "star," "flower" or "metal." "Art" is a word of evaluative suggestion and the consequence of this is that something may be rejected as "not a case of literary art" for two different reasons: it is not sufficiently like the kind of linguistic composition we would normally consider an unmistakable case of literary art, or, though it is similar in kind, it is not good enough to qualify. Thus there is linguistic composition that is nonliterary and linguistic composition that is subliterary. Moreover, the demarcation line between the literary and the nonliterary and between the literary and the subliterary is not sharp. This is the state of affairs which, from the theoretical point of view, can only be called troublesome.

Theory must strive for lucidity, but not at the price of relevance. The most lovely luminous theory will, after all, fail of its purpose if it slips its moorings, if it floats loose from the empirical data it is supposed to deal with and to clarify. Still, there is one consideration that may, to some extent, comfort us. Distinctions, in order to be useful, do not have to be sharp, knife-edge distinctions, just as evidence, in order to be evidence, does not have to be conclusive evidence. In all situations where we have "thing of the sort X" passing over through border-line cases to "thing of the sort Y," we can, at any rate, attempt to specify the salient characteristics of X and Y. Doubtful cases will then be doubtful because they are X-like in some respects but Y-like in others.

The distinction between the literary and the nonliterary should not be confused with the distinction between the literary and the subliterary. The latter must be evaluative; the former can be, at any rate to some extent, descriptive. The former distinction has a claim to logical priority, since the judgment "not good enough," means "not good enough as a certain sort of thing" so that it is only if we have some notion of the sort of thing involved that we can make this judgment. Let us, therefore, put aside the distinction between the literary and the sub-literary and turn our attention to the task of distinguishing between the literary and the nonliterary.

It is evident, surely, that not every linguistic composition presents itself as a case, or a possible case, of literary art. It is also evident, at least on a little reflection, that the judgment "not a candidate for consideration as a case of literary art" cannot be made on the basis of the query: Is it well-written? Ideally, everything written ought to be well-written. Suppose I draw up a list of instructions on how to assemble some object or on how to use a machine, and this contains everything necessary to be mentioned without ambiguity or redundancy and the mentioning is in the correct sequential order, then this is well-written. But, though it may be as well-written as it could possibly be, it is not, by any stretch of the imagination, what we would normally consider a work of literary art. Nor shall we find the distinction we seek by adding to the requirement "well-written," the additional proviso "well-written in a way that makes an aesthetic appeal." Supposing my initial draft of these instructions is to some extent confused, I revise it, I eliminate redundancy, I clear up ambiguity, I reorganize. Finally I have it as it should be, well-organized, lucid, and neat. Might I not derive aesthetic satisfaction from this well-formed structure? Surely I might.

It will be wise, I think, to recognize that the range of the aesthetic is far wider than the range of the artistic. We may expect some connection between the artistic and the aesthetic, but we certainly cannot say that everything that makes an aesthetic appeal is art. This is not simply because nature, natural objects, can elicit and reward

aesthetic regard, but that objects which are the product
of human activity can do this, too, without, for such reason, being considered works of art. A mathematical demonstration can be not only consistent but also elegant, and
"elegance" is surely an aesthetic term.

This is, perhaps, the point at which it may occur to
us to say: "Well, if the object is a human artifact, and if its
sole justification, its sole end or purpose, is to make an
aesthetic appeal, then this is art." But will this do if the
art we are thinking of is literary art? Certainly it will be
appropriate to expect that literary art will have something
in common with other arts, but is it not also a distinctive
art with special peculiarities of its own? Is it possible,
even if it were desirable, for an art that is *linguistic* to be
simply and solely an aesthetically alluring, lovely form?
In short, will a strictly formalistic view, such as may serve
appropriately for some works of nonliterary art, serve also
for literary art?

There are, indeed, theories about art that tend to as-
similate all the arts to the condition of literary art.
Through a stretched use of the word "language" one can
speak of "musical language" or "musical discourse." Discussion of style in visual art can make mention of "syn-
tax" and "vocabulary." Of course there is nothing wrong,
in principle, with the use of analogy; it would be simply
silly to prohibit analogy. But something additional, and
controversial, is involved if its use is intended to enforce
the claim that all art has the kind of meaning characteristic of language in the sense in which "language" denotes
specific languages such as French, Arabic, Spanish. Theories
that tend in the direction of regarding all art as somehow
"linguistic" can be matched by theories that tend in the
opposite direction. Art proper is now considered as purely
formal design of sensuous materials, and art is simply the
expression of the will to form. Since language, though it
can be rich in meaning, has little to offer in the way of di-

rect sensuous presence, literature, to be art, must somehow attempt to evade its linguistic condition. Perhaps it can be a kind of "verbal music" or "verbal painting" and, if it cannot quite succeed, then it cannot quite be art. But the question can be asked: Why should *any* distinctive art aspire to the condition of some other art? Why can it not be itself?

It is appropriate enough to expect that all the arts will exhibit some general resemblance, and it is also appropriate to look for this in a consideration of art-form or art-structure, but, since literary art is linguistic, the structure of a work of literary art must be a structure of linguistic meaning. The problem this poses is that, since *any* intelligible linguistic composition is a structure of such meaning, we must try to discern the difference between literary and nonliterary structure as preliminary to any inquiry into what kind of meaning literary art-structure is distinctively equipped to provide. Revision of writing, any kind of writing, can be undertaken primarily with the intent of stylistic improvement, and, up to a point, stylistic improvement can be secured without alteration of meaning, but however much stylistic improvement may render a linguistic composition more aesthetically acceptable, it does not for this reason make it art. Briefly put, literary art does not exist to "say things nicely" but to speak in some distinctive manner.

If it is structure that makes literary art similar to other art, it is language that makes it literary. To suppose that language is here a disability is surely fantastic. Literary art, since it is linguistic, can be said to be the most indirect of the arts but the question is not: How can the disadvantage of indirection be overcome? but, rather: How can the art of literature exploit the advantage of indirection? Every art must be considered to have its particular opportunities and resources. Sound, of course, plays a role in literature, particularly poetry, but sound divorced from sense has little of the effectiveness we are constantly tempted to ascribe to it. Consider, for example, "Rose of Castile" and "rows of cast steel." If language is meager from the point of view of what it has to offer in the way of direct sensuous presence, it is rich in range of reference. Language can evoke the sensuous, the emotional, and the intellectual, with equal facility. Though it would be an error to assert that a poem, or other work of literature, is always more complex in structure than, for example, a musical composition, it is not, I think, an error to assert that even a relatively simple work of literature embraces a greater diversity of different kinds of things— of elements derived from different levels or domains of experience—than could be accommodated in a work of nonlinguistic art. Otherwise expressed, literature lends itself to elaborations and complications of interpretation far more extensive than anything that can be—or that *need* be—provided by any other art. It is thus not a matter of accident, nor a matter of misplaced intellectualism, if the question of knowledge, understanding, or insight is raised in connection with literature as it need not be raised for all art. If this question arises it is not because literary art is less art but because it is a distinctive art. But it is one thing to see why a question arises and another thing to see how it can be answered. There is, I believe, a problem about this answer, and it is the character of literary art-structure that poses the problem.

The distinction, in linguistic composition, between the literary and the nonliterary is, I would suggest, best made by reference to total pattern of compositional design. It is possible to describe, in a general way, the difference between two types of pattern for linguistic composition, one of which can be called artistic and the other nonartistic. However, it must be acknowledged that this distinction can be brought out only by contrasting clear and manifest cases of each. There will be instances of writing that are difficult to classify, and of these it must simply be said that they are in some respect art-like and in some respect not. The simplest way to present the difference is to say that a linguistic composition is, or aspires to be, artistic in so far as it is nonteleological and moves towards *closure,* whereas it is nonartistic in so far as it is teleological and moves toward *conclusion.* Since we do, however, speak of the conclusion of a novel, poem or drama, it will be necessary to explain the meaning assigned to "conclusion" when conclusion is to be contrasted with closure.

The nonartistic ideal is the ideal of progressive development to a goal or end, and this is what is meant by calling it teleological. This end constitutes the element of prime importance for the sake of which everything else exists, and the structural pattern may be roughly symbolized by a line along which one moves. In the measure that this ideal is capable of being fulfilled, what is left behind is completely left behind, used up, exploited. If its import has been fully grasped, it may as well disappear, for its purpose is to bring the reader or writer to the place where he now is. When the goal or end is reached, it constitutes the prize, the fruition, the conclusion. Ideally, this conclusion is detachable and can provide the starting point for a new excursion. This pattern is most nearly approximated in anything that can be called a demonstration. Of course the road by which one arrives is of importance because, though arrival is the great thing, it will not be acknowledged as arrival unless it has been by the proper road. This is what persons have in mind when they say, with understandable but misleading exaggeration, that the method or the argumentation is everything. It is really the conclusion that is everything, provided its papers, so to speak, are all in order. This ideal is, often enough, only generally approximated, so that instead of a single line there is a network of lines, far from neat. Lack of neatness may be the failure of the writer or it may be necessitated by the kind of subject-matter with which the writer deals. However, the thing of importance to notice is that if the structure of the linguistic discourse is teleological, that is, directed towards a goal or end, and if the discourse moves forward, in however hesitant a fashion, to this end, it is the nonartistic ideal that prevails.

The artistic ideal is different. It is more properly symbolized by a circle than by a line, for the purpose is not to reach a conclusion but to achieve a total presentation. Of course this does not mean that there is no character of progression, for literary art necessarily has temporal order, and no literary artist who knows what he is about would neglect to exploit the temporal character of his art. We know that this can be done in a variety of ways, and that these differences in formal pattern have different expressive potentialities. Nevertheless, it can be said that no element in literary structure can attain its full significance until everything is present, for lines of reference and relationship do not all flow in one direction. Though the order of introduction of the various parts will certainly count for the total effect, yet it is the total effect that matters. When a literary critic refers to "the argument of a poem" he usually does not mean argument in the sense of argumentation; he means thematic development. To be sure there are poems that present the appearance of "arguing a case"—why the coy mistress should yield, or why death should not be proud—but the effect of rhetorical persuasiveness depends on everything in the poem, and this is not argument in the sense of argument to a detachable conclusion. If we think of demonstration as yielding something which, having been established, can provide the starting point for further inquiry, then this is not demonstration. Thus nonliterary linguistic composition, that moves towards conclusion, is distinguishably different from literary composition, that moves towards closure. The general difference between the two types of composition is comparable to the difference in experience between travelling along a road to a destination, on the one hand, and, on the other, exploring, though according to a controlled order of sequence, an enclosed garden.

This way of distinguishing the literary from the nonliterary is, I think, more comprehensive than other suggestions that have been made, but it need not be thought of as in opposition to these views. For instance, it has been remarked that what distinguishes the literary use of language is its greater exploitation of associative or suggestive meaning. A poem *says* more than it explictly *states*. Thus literature tends to have implicit meaning or, as it is often called, depth-meaning. It can be seen that this function of literary language consorts very well with the kind of compositional design I have distinguished as literary. For purposes of presentation, multiple meaning provides body, substance, richness; but for purposes of demonstration multiple meaning, now usually called ambiguity, is commonly an impediment. It interferes with the kind of precision nonliterary discourse aspires to have. To say one thing at a time, rather than several things, makes, of course, for thinness in language, but then, language, employed predominantly for passage to a conclusion, had perhaps, better be thin.

Coleridge said about poetry that it should provide such delight from the whole as is compatible with a distinct gratification from each component part, and other literary theorists have made somewhat comparable remarks about literary art in general. This, too, can be seen to consort well with the distinction, here proffered, between the literary and the nonliterary. *Any* kind of well-organized linguistic composition must, to be well-organized, relate the parts to the whole, but this can be done in different ways.

An art structure of any complexity is commonly a structure of substructures. This is the case whether the art structure be literary or not. Architects, in their discussion of architectural art, refer to what they call "an architectural member." This is an architectural substructure that can be considered for itself, for example, a doorway, a pediment, a tower, a spire. Of course the discernment of what in a particular case *is* an architectural member depends on the perceptive recognition of architectural style. For instance, a doorway must be especially displayed to count as an architectural member and in many New York skyscrapers the doorway is not. Now an art substructure can have a certain degree of autonomy. This is why a piece of fragmented sculpture, if fragmented in a certain way, providing, for example, a head or a torso, can have artistic as well as archeological importance. This remark about the possibility of relative autonomy for an art substructure may seem to be in conflict with another remark often made with reference to art, namely, that an art structure is a system of internal relationships so that every part is what it is because of its dependence on other parts. Yet we can, I think, say both. Every art critic who approaches the task of analyzing an art structure takes for granted two things. First of all, he assumes that it is only the art object itself that can reveal to him what, in any particular case, is a relatively autonomous substructure. Secondly, he assumes that, whatever be the relative autonomy of this structure, it is not completely autonomous. Though he may consider it for itself, he must also consider it as it functions in the total structure. Thus we are not really making incompatible assertions if we say with reference to a literary structure, that the full significance of any part depends on its functional role in the total presentation, but that, since in art-structure *all* parts are important, we expect to derive satisfaction and reward as we read.

It may be of interest to notice that, when we contrast clear cases of these two types of linguistic organization, the literary and the nonliterary, we can see them as structures made up of parts that resemble the whole. Just as relatively autonomous substructures in literary art structure can be regarded as little art achievements, so nonliterary discourse addressed to conclusion, but seeking to establish certain points as it goes along, will provide at intervals what can be thought of as little conclusions. Such little conclusions, though primarily intended as basis for further development, might recommend themselves as such and this is why we can say, with reference to such discourse, that we accept this or that even when we do not accept everything.

Before proceeding I think it will be necessary, at this point, to guard against a possible misapprehension that might be engendered by the extent to which, and the way in which, I have sought to contrast the literary with the nonliterary. This contrast should not, and need not, be interpreted to mean that any linguistic composition that is not unmistakably one or the other, but presents itself as border-line is, for this reason, bad. Writing that is not clearly literary art may need to be, in some respect, art-like to achieve its purpose. It is sometimes said that literary criticism should not itself be literature because *as* literature, it creates an object that is a substitute for, or a rival of, the art object which the discourse is ostensibly about. This can, of course, happen; yet it need not happen. A variety of rather different enterprises can be subsumed under the general title "literary criticism." Supposing, for example, the task in hand is to elicit appreciation for the new, the neglected, or for that which is alien because remote in time or culture. Strict analysis of parts will not suffice; there must be evocation of presence, and how is presence—distinct, individual presence—to be evoked except by the kind of writing that has some of the attributes of literary art? Then, again, consider the range of different enterprises subsumed under the term "history." If you pick up a volume with some such title as *The Causal Influence of Eco-*

nomic Factors in the American Civil War, you expect to find claim, and the marshaling of evidence in support of claim. This, then, will tend in the direction of the nonliterary. But suppose the title is *Life in a Cluny Monastery in the Twelfth Century.* If this is history it will be, or purport to be, informationally responsible. Still, if the enterprise is to convey the sense of what such life was like, the writer who can succeed with this must have more than information at his command; he must have something of the talent of the literary artist. The purist error of scorning what might be called "mixed modes," without any attempt to discern what purpose such mixture serves, should not, of course, be "corrected" by the erroneous view that mixture is a magical device for securing the best of everything. I think we can say, and say with assertive emphasis, that no defense can be made for the claim that there is some single kind of writing that is, from all points of view and for all purposes, *the* ideal.

In drawing this distinction between the literary and the nonliterary, I have attempted to offer a descriptive account of the characteristic. But the characteristic is not identical with the good. Whether or not something is characteristic is discoverable on inspection, but appraisal of goodness is never just a matter of simple inspection. To judge something to be border-line with respect to the distinction between the literary and the nonliterary is to describe it, but this does not settle the question of whether it is good for something to have this border-line status. To form an opinion we must try to discern the purpose in hand and also how well it has been carried out. But to say that something is semiliterary, or border-line, is not the same as saying that it is subliterary. The judgment that a linguistic composition is subliterary is a value judgment; to voice this judgment is not to describe but to condemn. If we think of the distinction between the literary and the nonliterary as approximately made along some horizontal line, we can think of the distinction between the literary and the subliterary as made, on the literary side, approximately along some vertical line. To employ both distinctions would be to indicate a region which, for all the admitted imprecision of its boundaries, would be the region of literary art proper.

The expression "work of literary art," as customarily used, has both descriptive and normative meaning. The evidence for this is that something might be rejected as "not a work of literary art" either on the ground that it is not characteristic enough or on the ground that it is not good enough. Any *full* answer to the question: What is literature? would have to take account of both meanings, but to attempt a full answer would be to develop a comprehensive theory that would not leave open and undecided the controversial issue of whether works of literary art can properly be said to have important cognitive import. It is the wish to leave this matter undecided that accounts for my initial concentration on descriptive meaning.

But though it is, I believe, both legitimate and useful to make a distinction between the characteristic and the good, the question can be raised as to whether it is really possible to provide a descriptive account of literature that will be *so* neutrally descriptive as not to suggest, in any way, a basis for evaluation. The candid answer must be that probably it is not. The reason for this is that works of literature are not found natural objects but man-made objects. The natural object, of a certain sort, may exhibit a characteristic structure, and we can ask why it has this structure. But, assuming the nonintervention of man, the answer to the question will be casual; it will be about the reciprocal causal interchange between this object and other natural objects. With respect to the man-made object, however, we can ask: What is the point of it? What are its possibilities? Accordingly, it has to be acknowledged that we

cannot completely eliminate all valuational suggestion
from a descriptive account. This state of affairs can be
brought out by considering the question of the subliterary.
In justifying the dismissal of something as subliterary, we
can distinguish general reasons from particular reasons. A
highly plausible general reason would be that the linguistic
composition makes so little of the possibilities, the intrinsic
potentialities, of the kind of thing it is. Thus *any* descriptive account designed to distinguish something as "a kind
of thing" will be likely to suggest how it might be good as
the particular kind of thing it is.

In the light of this acknowledgment, the question can
be raised as to whether the descriptive distinction between
the literary and the nonliterary, here proffered, really is
indecisive on the issue of literature and knowledge. The
distinction is, I believe, indecisive in that it does not *settle*
the matter. Nevertheless, what is indecisive can still be suggestive. But what this suggestion amounts to is that it may
perhaps be a mistake to look to literary art for anything
properly describable as knowledge. To cursory inspection,
it would seem that, if what we seek is knowledge, then it
is nonliterary linguistic structure that is most apt for the
purpose. Here we can find explicitly stated knowledge-
claims supported by argument, here we can find conclusion. *This* is the language of inquiry, and we may think of
knowledge as the fruit of inquiry. Literary linguistic structure which moves towards closure, rather than conclusion,
seems deliberately to defeat inquiry. A work of literature
has a kind of self-sufficiency, it seems to be important in
itself, it has none of the meek submissiveness characteristic
of linguistic discourse faithfully serving some end beyond
itself.

If, then, the descriptive account of literature which I
offer carries the suggestion that it may be a mistake to look
to literary art for anything that can appropriately be called
knowledge, this state of affairs is all to the good. It is all to

the good because I intend to argue for the opposite conclusion, and there is little interest in arguing for the obvious or for what has been prejudged by initial specification of meaning. I do believe, however, that *some* accounts of how literary art can be revelatory or cognitively significant, are unsatisfactory and I hope that the reader will be willing to give some initial attention to these views, for it is useful, after all, to understand why unsatisfactory views are unsatisfactory.

IV

Vehicle and Image

A WORK of literary art might be thought to have revelatory import or cognitive significance either as the vehicle of some warranted empirical claim, or as an illuminating image. According to the first view, we ask: What does the work of literature assert or claim? According to the second, we ask: What does it show forth or exhibit? These approaches are sufficiently different to require independent consideration.

I

If we ask: Can we regard a work of literature as the vehicle of a claim, a message, a thesis of some sort? the answer would seem to be that, in almost all cases, we can. We can, but should we? This is a different question. If it be the case that literary art has some intimate engagement with knowledge, will it be appropriate to find this in the form of some warranted claim for which the work of literature is a vehicle? If, in speaking of literary insight, revelation or disclosure, we have in mind something which literary art is *distinctively* equipped to provide, then the answer must be no.

Yet however unsatisfactory the vehicle view of literature may be, it will be worth while to grant it a brief examination, for it may be useful to have a more thorough understanding of why it will not do. In order to consider a work of literature from this point of view, two questions must be raised: first, can we find, in a work of literature, some sort of claim? secondly, if we can, how do we assess the warrantability or truth of this claim?

Literature abounds in declarative sentences, but surely it may be presumed that no reader in his right mind would think of regarding *every* declarative sentence he meets in a work of literature as the statement of a claim that calls for assessment as true or false, right or wrong. A figure of speech he will naturally take as an invitation to a manner of apprehension rather than as a propositional claim. Whether life, compared to a dome of colored glass, does or does not stain the white radiance of eternity is a question no one asks. It may also be assumed that all narrative assertions concerning situations, events, and fictional characters, will be accepted as given. The horseman on the moor, the ghost on the battlement, the dragon in the forest, are all present as stated. This is just the natural recogniton by the reader that the given is given to be taken. It is not until we encounter what might be called reflective generalizations that the temptation first arises to suppose that we are confronted by an empirical claim calling for assessment.

Anna Karenina opens with the remark: "All happy families are alike, every unhappy family is unhappy in its own way." Probably few, if any, readers will be likely to pause over this and ask themselves: Is it so? The reader will more likely simply await the implicitly promised account of the unhappy family in its particular way of being unhappy. But should this, or any other generalization, appear as a kind of summing up, or as the single assertion of some relatively autonomous substructure in a complex work of literature, it might then perhaps be taken as a straightforward empirical claim. So long as we are content simply to quote it, on what seems to us some appropriate occasion, or so long as we are content to compile anthologies in the form of "gems of wisdom gleaned from the poets," we may never recognize the full consequences of taking such literary statements as direct empirical claims. The only way to recognize this is to be rigorous in such taking and observe the unfortunate consequences.

Consider this from John Webster:

> Vain the ambition of kings,
> Who seek by trophies and dead things
> To leave a living name behind,
> And weave but nets to catch the wind.

If we are to take this seriously as an empirical claim we must ask: Is it the case that the hope or expectation on the part of kings for posthumous remembrance is always delusive? The answer seems to be, certainly not. We all remember Alexander the Great, Caesar Augustus, Charlemagne, Louis XIV. Ah, but what the poem says is that it is vain if it is sought through the instrumentality of "trophies and dead things." What does this mean? If all that a king can leave behind him is a monument, he will not long be remembered? Perhaps. Certainly "dead things," whatever they may be, will be likely to be inefficacious. Inefficacious means to an end will not be effective. This is, indeed, a necessary truth by virtue of linguistic convention.

Obviously something seems to be wrong here, but is it the rough treatment accorded the poem or the assumption that invites that treatment? It is surely the latter. Given the assumption, what choice have we except to subject such claims to the same scrutiny to which anything purporting to be an empirical claim must submit? The consideration of additional examples will not mend the matter, for any explicitly stated reflective generalization in literature will be likely to be mishandled by this method. The point is not that any such generalization, considered as claim, is un-

warranted if presumed empirical. There is nothing whatever to prevent a poet from telling us that the leaves fall in
the autumn or that time seems longer when one is a child,
or anything else that we would accept without question.
The logical point of the matter is that the whole appearance of cognitive importance which attaches to explicitly
stated reflective generalizations depends on their not being
trite but, on the contrary, interesting if true, and it is this
conditional "if," taken seriously, that makes for mischief.
We all know, simply on the basis of casual conversation,
that many an arresting generalization quickly collapses into
error or triteness if we press the query: Always or just
sometimes? In most cases or in some cases?

But the view that works of literature are appropriately
regarded as vehicles of knowledge-claims is not so easily
disposed of. It may be thought that any embarrassments so
far encountered are owing to the error of seeking such
claims in explicit and isolated statements. It might be said
that the significant claim is implicit rather than explicit,
and necessarily so because it is something that emanates
from the totality of the literary structure.

Something, of course, does so emanate. The knowledge-
able and sensitive reader achieves gradual awareness of a
total emergent presence generated by language but tran-
scending specific statement. But we still have to ask
whether what so emerges, or any part of it, may be con-
strued as something presented for consideration as warranted or unwarranted. We can hardly suppose that there
is such a claim unless we can state the claim. Accordingly,
what must happen is first the eliciting of theme, and then
the eliciting of claim from theme or the stating of theme
as claim. Now it seems that this can be done; something of
the sort has, in fact, often been attempted by critics. What is
troublesome here is not any doubt about the propriety of
the critical interest in elucidating a theme for, assuming
the success of the critic, how can it be other than helpful to

have our attention directed to the thematic structure of a
work of literature? Furthermore, thematic structure may
reasonably be thought of as something more general than
narrative or dramatic structure in that it seems to emerge
as some sort of general "point of view" and it may, therefore, appear neither inappropriate nor unnatural to state
this general point of view directly as claim, for to do so is
to bring it out in an arresting fashion. But we shall need to
ask how we are to take this claim. Is it something that may
be considered on its own merits and debated as such? Is it
proper to consider it as the message of the work of literature? Surely to take it thus will be productive of embarrassments. We must ask: What is the point of its being
implicit?

Let us look at the matter this way. Aesop is easy. He
gives us the story or fable and then appends a moral or
message. Here is the claim explicitly stated, and here is
the supporting "evidence" in the form of an illustration.
But if the Aesopic fable is not regarded as the ideal of literary achievement, is this simply that what is easy is tiresome? Is it to be pleasing or teasing that literary artists are
evasive?

The question of importance is not whether it is possible to elicit and so, of course, to state explicitly, some
general claim that may be said to operate implicitly in a
work of imaginative literature. This can be done, at least
in many cases. The question is how do we interpret this
claim? What do we do with it? How do we use it? One
possibility is to say: "Such and such is the state of affairs
in the imaginative world of the work; these are the valuational attitudes, these are the assumptions about the condition of man or the world; all this is how things are *there*.
To have this summed up and explicitly stated may be useful in helping the reader to find his way in the work of literature." But something quite different is involved if we
say: "This is the claim made by the work of literature, or

by its author, about man and the world, this is the revelatory import."

A possible claim about the human condition, elicited and explicitly stated might run as follows: "We delude ourselves if we suppose that we can find our freedom and our self-realization by the path of withdrawal from the intimacy of human relationships. This isolation, far from providing fulfillment, results in impoverishment. Only through generous participation in the life of others can we be ourselves." There, now, is something big and possessing an air of impressiveness: the essence of wisdom concerning the human condition. Or so it seems until we fall under the spell of the next work of literature. But the claim elicited from the next work is somewhat different. "We delude ourselves if we suppose that we can ever really enter with any intimacy into the life of others. The more seemingly intimate the relationship the more inescapable the realization that every man is, in fact, an island unto himself. On the honesty, courage, and dignity with which we accept this hard and terrible truth depends all personal integrity, all civilization, all courtesy." It seems as if every claim might have its counter-claim and, in so far as we suspect this, we become uneasily aware that we approach the land of proverbs. This is the land where the sign says: "Look before you leap, but remember, he who hesitates is lost."

If works of literature are vehicles of knowledge-claims, and are to be taken seriously, knowledge-claims then must also be taken seriously, which is to say that collision of such claims must be taken seriously. This is the point, I suppose, at which someone may wish to say: "Well, the author, after all, is just presenting his opinion and everyone is entitled to his own opinion." But we have to ask: What is an opinion? Is it something that can be presumed to be private property? Is my opinion like my dog, my house, my books? An opinion is a claim, and it is inherent in the very nature of opinion to be open to question. Surely it can be nothing but an elementary muddle to confuse the right of a person to have and to express an opinion with the rightness of the opinion. Oddly enough the remark "It's a matter of opinion" is sometimes said with the idea of closing off controversy. Yet since what this remark actually means is "the issue is controversial," why should it not be appropriate to suggest that we proceed directly to the controversy?

The assumption that a work of literary art is essentially the vehicle of some general claim will have the effect of bringing literature into direct competition with every other form of linguistic discourse concerned with claim, and in this competition literature must show to disadvantage. Nothing can prevent the rise of the embarrassing question: What is there to back this claim, where is the evidence, where is the argument, what reasons are there to suppose that this claim is warranted? To be without credentials is awkward. Nor will it do to suggest that absence of credentials is to be explained by originality of discovery. Not, that is, if discovery is considered to be discovery of something capable of being expressed in the form of a generalized claim. Supposing we try the gambit of saying that literary artists are prophets and seers in that they somehow glimpse general truths that less inspired and more pedestrian inquirers, plodding along in the disciplines of natural or social science, can later verify. Such a view asks us to consider works of literature as vehicles of hypotheses, but it is surely impossible to regard anything as an hypothesis without having a lively interest in how it fares with respect to test, without wishing to know what the verdict concerning confirmation or reputation may turn out to be. This verdict must be supplied on the basis of some non-literary inquiry. Let us ask: Do literary artists, do lovers of literature, wait with concern for news about verdicts as supplied by scientists or historians? They do not. Is the past history of literature, like the past history of science, strewn with the debris of unsuccessful hypotheses? No. If literary artists are prophets they are more likely to be prophets in the sense in which prophets are those who "speak with tongues." Prophets, in this sense, produce effects rather than predict states-of-affairs.

The basic difficulty of the vehicle view of literary art is that it requires us to distinguish a cognitive claim from a linguistically alluring garment in which it is, in some way, clothed. Since it takes only a little reflection to recognize that this garment, no matter how alluring, will not suffice to justify the truth of the cognitive claim, we must suppose that its function is to convey the claim persuasively, in short, literature teaches through pleasing. Readers of literature are those who, because of some sort of mental incapacity, cannot be expected to take their teaching straight and must, therefore, be beguiled, and literary artists are specialists in this beguilement. On such a view, Platonic alarm is far more justified than Horatian complacency.

II

To turn from the vehicle view of literature to the conception of a work of literary art as a representational or mimetic image is to turn in the direction of greater adequacy. We now abandon the question: What does a work of literature claim? and ask instead: What does it exhibit, show forth, or display? The notion of a work of literature as an image has two obvious advantages: it accounts for the function of narrative or dramatic structure and it makes evident why the literary artist must be creative. These are, of course, related. An image must be other than that of which it is an image, and must, therefore, be constructed or "made," for, if an image is an image by virtue of similarity, it is also such by virtue of difference. Representation can be understood as re-presentation, presentation with a difference. It might be argued that the whole possibility of revelatory display depends on the interplay between similarity *and* difference, so that it is open to anyone deploying this theory to make as much as he needs to of the factor of difference.

The view of a work of literature as a constructed, created, imaginative world of character, scene, event seems most obviously applicable to the novel, the story, the drama, the epic, but it is a view that can be extended to include the lyrical poem, for here there is at least one character, the speaker of the poem, some scene or setting and some event, even if this be no more than a meditation on the part of the speaker. Assuming the propriety of this extension, and thus the generality of the description of a work of literature as an imaginative world, we can turn to the examination of the implications of this view. The minimum implication would be that of some semblance between the imaginative world of character, scene, event, and the actual world of person, place and occurrence. We go beyond this minimum if, in addition to resemblance, we also assume reference. It is important to notice that mere resemblance by no means insures reference. In the actual world of our ordinary experience we constantly note resemblance of one thing to another without any temptation to claim that one refers to the other, as when we observe that one person resembles another or that one state-of-affairs is similar to another. Accordingly, the mere fact of some resemblance between what we encounter in a work of literary art and the world beyond does not of itself justify the claim to reference. If this assumption is to be made, it must be established on the basis of additional considerations.

Are there such considerations? It would seem that there must be some, for certainly the tendency to suppose reference is fairly prevalent. If reference is relevant, the issue of truth arises again, but in shifting the emphasis from the view of literature as "discourse about," to that of literature as mimesis, the question of truth is also changed from the notion of "true about" to that of "true to." Only a claim can be true about, but a presentation can be true to. Accordingly, we must ask: Is it sensible to regard literary semblances as referential, and, if so, in what sense is it appropriate to expect that they should be true to life, human experience, nature, the world, or whatever?

Nature, including of course human nature, is prior to literature; and acquaintance with it is a necessary requirement for both the making and the understanding of a literary semblance. Moreover, the creation of a literary, or for that matter a pictorial, semblance does not seem to be the making of something which, once made, becomes an addition to "the furniture of the world." New things arise in nature and new things are made by man, but mimetic-making, art-semblance making, is in an important respect not like shoe-making or ship-making. We can say appropriately that art is invention, but it is not inventoin in the sense in which the telescope and the internal combustion machine are inventions. These latter, once invented, become "things-in-the-world," absorbed, so to speak, into the inclusive spatial-temporal-causal nexus of actuality. The art object, considered as mimetic, is different. It has, indeed, some sort of public presence in the world, but though *in* the world, it is not *of* it. It is closed-off, isolated, set apart. This is what has been remarked as its air of "otherness." Pictorial space is distinguishable from actual space, that is, the space occupied by the extension of the canvas. The imaginative world of a work of literature is no section, segment, or continuous part of natural, actual life experience. When we return to take up our interrupted reading of a work of literature, we pass out of one world into another. Thus, oddly enough, the autonomy of the literary art work, the very thing that might suggest its nonreferential independence, can also suggest this reference. In short, since it is not "a part of the world" it might present itself as "an image of the world."

But in what sense is it an image? Any plausible account of a resemblance that also involves a reference must take account of difference in two respects: the difference between one work of literature and another, and the difference between any work of literature and the actual world. To speak of a work of literature as "an imaginative world" is to acknowledge not simply its separation from the context of actuality, but also its separation from other works of literature. To be sure, the literary works of a single author may display sufficient similarity to allow us to think of them as aspects of a single imaginative world, but we have only to consider works by different authors to recognize that the scene of every work of literature is not only "another part of the island" but that there may be no topography of this island in the sense that there is no passage of a kind that would permit Dostoevsky's Underground Man to appear for tea at a Trollope parsonage.

As I have already noted, revelatory disclosure might be regarded as a product of the interplay between difference and similarity, so that if we turn our attention to the difference between any work of literature and the actual world, we might say that there is some sort of noncorrespondence that functions to make possible a correspondence on another level. There is a passage in the *Republic* where Socrates attacks all forms of representational art, whether pictorial or literary, on the ground that such representation is a copy of something in nature which is itself a copy of the higher reality of the Ideas, and goes on to say that this kind of image-making is a trick that anyone can perform by holding up a mirror and turning it about. However, "holding the mirror up to nature" is susceptible of another interpretation, for it might be said that this art-mirror is no ordinary mirror.

In the *Poetics* Aristotle says that the poet is under no obligation to report what actually happened, and there is the suggestion that the poet can turn this freedom to account by presenting something which, though false on one level, can be true on another. There is the famous remark that poetry is more philosophic than history. Some lovers of literature have been happy to quote this remark, but lovers of literature, like lovers in general, may be subject to the temptation to accept with alacrity any pronouncement about the object of their devotion that seems to be a compliment. We have to consider exactly what this claim amounts to, for it is by no means obvious that poetry is praised in being said to approach the condition of something other than itself.

Here is the relevant passage: "Hence poetry is more philosophic and of a graver import than history, since its statements are of the nature rather of universals, whereas those of history are singulars. By a universal statement I mean one as to what such and such a kind of man will probably or necessarily say or do—which is the aim of poetry, though it affixes proper names to the characters; by a singular statement, one as to what, say, Alcibiades did or had done to him." (*Poetics*, 1451b, trans. W. D. Ross.)

Now as an answer to the complaint that the art image is a mere copy of a copy, this has its relevance. If it be supposed that history is just chronicle, the straightforward factual report of sequential events, then drama can be more intelligible in presenting the characteristic, the typical, the representative. It is in exhibiting such generality that poetry is more philosophic than history.

To be sure, some literary theorists have been a little uneasy with this, so much so that they have wished to say that Aristotle could not have meant just the characteristic but something presumably more subtle and impressive, namely, "the presentation of the universal in the particular." But since for Aristotle the universal is simply the com-

mon character of particular like things, that by virtue of
which they can be grouped and classified, the representative case is precisely what the text suggests it would be
appropriate to look for in literary presentation.

What is necessary for a mimetic presentation of "men
in action" is the probable, the probable as we might be expected to recognize it on the basis of our common experience, in other words, verisimilitude. Since some sort of
verisimilitude is, in fact, a necessary ingredient in all works
of literature, we shall be dissatisfied with this only if we
hold the view that impressive works of literary art can provide a revelatory insight more significant than mere verisimilitude. In fairness to Aristotle it must be remembered
that he does not specify the end of literature as insight
but as pleasure. No doubt part of this pleasure is the pleasure of recognition. We can be delighted in a mimetic representation simply as such. But this is by no means the
whole story. If the only truth the literary artist need be expected to provide is the truth of verisimilitude, then the
artist is free to shape the mimetic presentation into a well-
formed structure, having beginning, middle, and end, and,
at least in the case of tragic art, to provide for emotive effect, for catharsis. In short, if this is a theory about literary
art that does not stress insight, it seems hardly reasonable
to complain that it does not provide for it.

However, as we know, the *Poetics* has had an enormous
influence on literary theory and has led to all sorts of quarrels about the role of the universal and the particular in
literary presentation, and although it is a matter of historical courtesy not to hold Aristotle responsible for all
these quarrels, yet something needs to be said about them
in order to clear the ground for further inquiry.

Let us first of all consider the place of verisimilitude
in literary presentation. The recognition of how a man of a
certain sort would act, or think, or feel, in a situation of
a certain sort is not irrelevant to literature. Some kind of

verisimilitude is an ingredient in *any* narrative or dramatic presentation, for it is the nature of literary art that the artist must remind us of what we already know, or must be able to assume what we already know, as a basis for new disclosure, if there be new disclosure. The kind of verisimilitude that a work of literature must have is predominantly humanistic verisimilitude. As far as physical events are concerned, very odd things may take place without disturbance of the literary illusion; what is necessary is that human reactions to events should seem plausible.

Our sense of what is plausible in this way is derived from our general life experiences and there is, naturally, a difference between the acquired expectations of the adult and the child. But the child will insist on this kind of verisimilitude in so far as the presented situation falls within the range of his experience. "Once upon a time there was a king who lived in a golden castle on the edge of a forest and in this forest there lived a dragon." If the story, thus begun, goes on to recount the establishment of a relation of friendship between the king and the dragon and later introduces an officious knight who incontinently kills the dragon and comes to boast of his achievement to the king, and it is said or suggested that the king does not care, we must expect instant protest. "Oh but the king would be angry, the king liked the dragon!" What operates in this simple case will operate in all cases. But the point to be made about this kind of elementary verisimilitude is that it is an ingredient in the most banal works of literature as well as the most impressive. Imagine a story, as trite as may be, about an adolescent girl who feels socially insecure but who longs for popularity, who comes to regard an invitation to a party as a test case of the longed-for success or the dreaded failure, who at some point is forced to recognize that she will not be invited and who suffers, in consequence, an acute distress. Is this true to life? Well, of course it is. No one doubts it, but who would seriously seek the revelations of literature in the obvious truth of such verisimilitude? If this story is trite, it is, of course, not the theme but the treatment that makes it such; the point that needs to be brought out, however, is that banal treatment is perfectly compatible with this kind of obvious truth. It is not that literary art can dispense with it, for it is necessary even in the most impressive literary creations. The distressing character of sexual jealousy is not irrelevant to *Othello,* it is just that it would be odd to dwell on "how true it is" that Othello should find it such.

The manifest falsity of fictional invention, the recounting of what, in point of fact, never happened, and the trivial truth of verisimilitude, the adherence to the probable, as we might be presumed to judge it on the basis of common experience, may both be seen to have a role in mimetic art; but if we are to speak of significant insight, revelation, epiphany, or disclosure, we must surely be concerned with something additional, very likely not simply additional but different.

The question now to be considered is whether anything of importance is to be discovered in this talk about the universal and the particular. What sense, if any, can be made of the claim that literature "presents the universal in the particular"? This will require a brief excursion into metaphysical dispute and the literary theories derived from it.

The whole vexed issue over generality and particularity, what is now customarily referred to as "the problem of universals," is difficult enough as a question of logic; it is many times more unmanageable as an object of passion. But it is a matter of historical record that this issue generated, and for centuries, an extraordinary amount of passion. Philosophers testified to their belief in universals almost as one might testify to belief in God. Other philosophers repudiated them with a vehemence more appropriate to the repudiation of the Devil and all his works. This behavior seems very puzzling if we consider that *blueness* and *treeness* might be cited as examples of universals. Why should anyone rise up to testify to the faith that is in him concerning *blueness?* Even more mysterious, why should anyone find it necessary to repudiate it? So long as we find this behavior fantastic we can be sure that we do not understand how the issue was regarded by those who felt the need for some sort of radical commitment on the matter.

The question seemed to be: What is Reality? This is not the same as: What is real? for this latter is a question that calls aloud for context—real in what way? real by reference to what concern, what interest? The pink rats seen by the delirious patient are unreal as biological animals though, of course, they are real enough as objects of the poor fellow's apprehension. Lower-case reality is a matter of relevance in context of interest, but the minds of men have been haunted by the idea of upper-case Reality. All discourse on the theme of appearance and reality involved talk about appearances, which were scrutinized and described; and this suggests that the appearances had their own kind of reality. But not so if to be Real means to be important, fundamental, basic. This is a value judgment that may very well evoke feeling.

Aristotle was, indeed, critical of the views of "the Platonists" but it is not until we encounter the nominalists of the twelfth century that we find the full oppositional contrast. We are then informed that universals have only a linguistic mode of being; they are merely general terms. All classifications are matters of convenience and to reify general terms as entities is to forsake things for words. But nominalism as a faith and a passion is still sustained by the haunting idea of upper-case Reality. What is Real is what exists and what exists is particular. Something of this metaphysical fervor passed over into critical theory by way of the assumption that literature, in some manner, exhibits Reality.

Anyone acquainted with the history of critical theory can recall the several controversies over the issue of generality versus specificity. The generality of the Grand Style which did not descend to "numbering the streaks of the tulip" seemed more noble and dignified as well as more illuminating, but, on the other hand, the specific, the concrete, made its appeal as being lively and vigorous; and since, in fact, streaked tulips do exist, the sponsors of the specific could associate the attraction of liveliness with the claim to truth. Controversies of this sort, controversies where it seems that there is something to be said on both sides, generate a familiar temptation, the temptation to suppose that there is some middle ground where wisdom resides—in this case the temptation to believe that there is some "optimum balance" between generality and specificity that would show as right or best for literary presentation. However, middle-ground-temptation, to give it a label, should be carefully scrutinized, for what is sensible in politics, for example, may prove to be silly in art. Compromise may very well be the basis on which we live, but compromise does not sound like anything on which art can live.

The advocacy of generality or the advocacy of specificity can amount to no more than the advocacy of some literary style, and whereas it is appropriate enough to consider the question of the expressive potentialities of different literary styles, we surely know, at least on the basis of a little reflection, that individual works of literature can succeed or fail according to the pattern of any recognizable style. The circumstantial detail of a realistic style may "number the streaks of the tulip" but whether this is a good thing or not cannot be judged except by reference to the internal economy of the individual work, for only so can we see what this counting comes to. The abstract generality of allegory cannot be said to be bad as such; allegory is simply a literary genre that may happen to be out of fashion at a particular time. It is necessary to move out of the shadow cast by the tree of Porphyry. The tree of Porphyry is a schematized system for the ordering of terms, an ordering of broader or narrower classes. For example, the class of animal is narrower than the class of animate things, and the class of rational animal is narrower than the class of animal. All this is sensible enough, and it is something we take account of in every use of language; what is not sensible is the scrambling up and down the tree of Porphyry in the vain hope of finding some suitable perch, branch, or position that will show as "just right" for literary presentation. The *Everyman* of literature has no place on the tree of Porphyry; to suppose that he has is to suppose that the introduction of a sufficient train of judiciously selected qualifying adjectives could transform him into, shall we say, Mr. Pickwick.

For theoretical purposes we need to have some clear understanding of what might be meant by this often repeated phrase "the presentation of the universal in the particular." We can begin with the question: Are we using the phrase to describe the general character of something we find *in* works of literary art, namely, simile, metaphor, symbol; or are we using it to describe the relationship between a work of literature, considered as a totality, and the world beyond? Certainly it is a theoretical possibility that we may mean both, in that the recognition of the former does not preclude the further, additional recognition of the latter. Even so, it will be necessary to deal separately and sequentially with these two possibilities.

If, for the purposes of this immediate context, I may be permitted to use the term "literary symbol" in a somewhat extended sense to include all cases of figures of speech, simile as much as symbol proper, then it can be said that literary symbol operates to relate or combine something derived from one level or domain of experience with something derived from another. Its structure is vertical. Ac-

cordingly, *any* analysis of a literary symbol can be expected
to reveal the interplay between something relatively concrete and something relatively abstract. That which is relatively concrete can be called "particular," and that which is
relatively abstract, "universal," and the total structural pattern can be called "the presentation of the universal in the
particular." It is to be noted, though, that this, just in itself, says nothing about the literary merit of a literary
symbol. It is also to be noted that the recognition of the
function of symbol *in* a work of literature by no means involves the assumption that literary art has, in fact, any relation of reference beyond itself to the trans-literary. But
if we are to keep to the mimetic theory we must suppose a
reference of some sort.

Let us, therefore, turn to the consideration of the meaning this phrase, about the particular and the universal,
might have as a device for describing the relation of a work
of literature, considered as a totality, to the world beyond.
Only a little reflection should be necessary to tell us that
any narrative or dramatic structure will have *some* particularity of presentation and, if it be intelligible at all, will
have *some* generality of reference. This, then, is something we do indeed find, but something we can scarcely
avoid finding. Perhaps it may be thought that I am bringing up rather heavy artillery to demolish the phrase "the
presentation of the universal in the particular," but this
phrase has about it a certain air of impressiveness, and so
long as it is allowed to retain this appearance it may seem
to provide a justifiably conclusive explanation of how works
of literary art can be revelatory.

The argument so far, if accepted as cogent, will not be
decisive on the general issue of literature and knowledge.
All that has been attempted is to show that the theory that
works of literary art can be cognitively illuminating will
not be worth much if it merely deals with the obvious. But
perhaps the notion of literature as "revelatory of life" and

of successful works of literary art as meeting something rather vaguely referred to as "the test of life" is susceptible of some more subtle and satisfactory account. Can it be that the revelations of literature are discovered in literature and not discoverable without benefit of literature, but that, nevertheless, our recognition of these revelations is dependent on some sort of awareness derived from life, although this awareness lies deeper than anything that could be described as "common sense opinions about the way of the world"? This is a possibility that must be explored.

V

Triumphant Intelligibility

IF works of literary art can be revelatory, this revelatory disclosure must be associated with literary impressiveness, for there would be no point in stressing cognitive illumination or insight in any theory of literature unless we suppose that this disclosure is something won through creative effort, and expressed through an exploitation of the artistic resources of the linguistic medium. The composition that we dismiss as trivial or banal may be perfectly intelligible in one accepted sense of the word, but dismissal on such ground, whether justified in any particular instance or not, would be the sign that what we seek in literary art is not mere intelligibility but something more properly described as triumphant intelligibility. Yet if triumphant intelligibility is considered to be a matter not simply of internal coherence and consistency, but of disclosure based on conformity or correspondence between literary art and something trans-literary, then anyone who would claim such disclosure must face up to skeptical doubts concerning its possibility.

Skeptical doubts about the availability of something vaguely referred to as "the test of life" can be elicited by the consideration that our sense of the impressiveness of a work of literature seems to be engendered not so much by "going to and fro in the world and walking up and down in it" like the Devil himself, as by extensive travel in the realm of literature. It seems also to be the case that when we are confronted by the admirer of the banal poem, we are more likely to ask: How much poetry have you read? than: How much experience of life have you had? We usually try to alter appraisal, not by inviting someone to consider the events of his experience or the significance of life, but by inviting him to consider other, in some way comparable, works of literature. We behave like Hamlet and say "look upon this" and then "look upon this." All such considerations tempt us to conclude that what determines literary judgment is not so much what life *is* as what literature *can be*.

If we are to give due weight to these considerations, as surely we should, then the assumption that there is something called "the test of life" that we can bring to the consideration of literature must be carefully considered. The difficulty involved might be stated as follows. If revelatory disclosure is something we discover *in* literature, so that literary experience is essential for its discovery, how can we say that our recognition of it *as* revelatory is dependent in any way on trans-literary life experience?

Perhaps it may be thought that there is no problem here, that it is gratuitous to suppose that there is anything that calls for explanation. Why should we not say something such as the following: we discover the revelatory insight in the work of literature and we just know that this is an insight into life, and we know, not by any process of deliberate inquiry or "testing out," but directly by the shock of recognition? The answer, I think, is that although this account of the matter may describe the character of our literary experience we might still wish to understand how this is possible. The shock of recognition, the "Ah-yes feeling," when "Ah!" is discovery and "Yes!" is confirmation, can be acknowledged as an occurrence and yet present itself as something that calls for explanation. The task of theory is to explain how something can be greeted as *both* revelatory *and* right, both "Ah!" and "Yes!" Perhaps an explanation can be found if we suppose that the trans-literary experience we draw upon for confirmation of rightness lies at a level far deeper than anything that can be thought of as formulated opinion.

Let us, for the moment, look away from literature and consider a kind of common remark that we must all have heard. Someone says: "Wouldn't you know, it has to be the son of the man with whom I quarreled so bitterly long ago in another country, that my daughter wishes to marry." This meets with the response: "Ah yes! That's life for you." Remarks of this sort are not "queer" in the sense that we would be astonished to hear them, but if we reflect upon them we can see that there is a sense in which they are odd. "Wouldn't you know" certainly cannot mean "wouldn't you naturally expect," and, "that's life for you" certainly cannot mean "this is the kind of thing that usually happens." What lies behind these remarks is a sense of something far deeper than any acquired empirical knowledge about the customary and the usual, for no one supposes that the state of affairs reported *is* the customary and the usual.

"Life," as it figures here, is something enigmatic and unmanageable. We may think that we can capture this Chimera in our nets of theoretical explanation, we may suppose that it will obediently conform to our elaborated plans for practical action, but our confidence is not deep, for this Chimera is, or at any moment can be, recalcitrant. It is impossible to foresee or to make provision for the brute obduracy of contingent fact. In the tropic domain of actuality too many things are going on at the same time. A vast multiplicity of independent entities pursue their individual destinies, but this independence is not complete, for lines of causal development, having different ancestry in the past, can cross, merge, collide, and when this happens we have an event that is contingent, that is fortuitous, in the particular sense that it appears as alien to the "system" of any of these purposive tendencies. Something of all of this, no doubt more felt than formulated, is what lies behind the remark "That's life for you!" This sense of "life" is not to be summed up in empirical generalizations about the customary and the characteristic. It is deeper, it is, in no pejorative meaning, more primitive.

The basic and primitive awareness of the recalcitrant life-chimera is something that, beyond childhood, we all have. It is experience and not literature that accounts for this. Nevertheless, the recognition of its accommodation in a work of literature is not available to everyone. This is because the provision is achieved by literary means, and the order is a literary order not easily "read off." It is only upon the basis of funded knowledge of past literary achievements that we are in a position to greet a new and another triumph. Thus it remains the case that although the recognition and the greeting involves a reference to something trans-literary, the reference would never have been made except as a consequence of developed literary experience. If we suppose that "poems are imaginary gardens with real toads in them" we must say that without the imaginary garden we would never have seen the toad. When we see him we recognize him, but there can be no seeing and no recognition without some trained capacity to find our way in this garden.

Certainly some works of literature would seem to be impressive and triumphantly intelligible because of an ordering of oppositional forces, something that we might call dramatic tension without implying that this is confined to drama or even always found there. The point of the phrase "dramatic tension" is that impressive works of literature in this mode are concerned with oppositional contrast, with paradox, with yes-and-no-ness. The "yes" of the reader's confirmation is a yes to the yes-and-no-ness displayed in the work of literature.

We cannot hope for intelligibility unless we have order, but the order of impressive works of literature in the mode of dramatic tension is an order in which some element of the inexplicable, of the recalcitrant, of the obdurate, of the unmanageable, is preserved and makes itself felt. The literary artist who can succeed with this must have what Keats called "negative capability"—the capacity to hold disparate elements in mind without irritable hankering after the simplicity of reduction, without hankering for dissolution in explanation. Negative capability is a certain kind of robustness of mind difficult if not impossible for those who are commonly called "thinkers." Thinkers are intent on explanation, but the triumph of literary intelligibility in the mode of dramatic tension depends upon restraint in explanation. It depends, indeed, upon a marvelously achieved combination of boldness and restraint—boldness in inclusion and restraint in explanation. On quick first consideration it may seem a little odd to say that restraint in explanation can play a role in the intelligibility of a work of literature, yet a little reflection suggests that this is warranted. Without such restraint we would not be impressed by the accommodating power of the presentation, and it is this that gives it its "air of reality" and elicits from the reader the response: "Ah yes! That's life for you."

The modern critical practice of close reading and analytical explication has directed our attention to complexities of multiple meaning, particularly in the form of oppositional contrast, ambivalence of attitude, the yes-and-no-ness of dramatic tension. This has had the salutary effect of persuading readers to desist from demanding that a work of literature should yield some sort of general conclusion in the form of an abstractable claim. It was once objected to Shakespeare that he lacked a "philosophy of life," some sort of general ideology. Shakespeare, however, is Keats' prime example of "negative capability," and this absence of hankering for reductive explanation is not unrelated to the power of accommodation and the air of reality characteristic of the plays.

No withdrawal or abatement of admiration for such literary achievements is implied by the suggestion, which I now make, that triumphant intelligibility in the mode of dramatic tension is not the only kind possible to literary art. The toad in the imaginary garden need not be the recalcitrant life-chimera. He can be a creature of such particular "suchness" that no amount of previous life experience can quite prepare us for the surprise of our encounter with him. Yet this surprise can also be the shock of recognition. The "Ah!" can be directly followed by the "Yes," though now we are not so likely to say "That's life for you" as "That's exactly it!" There are impressive works of literature that are impressive, not so much by reason of comprehensive yes-and-no inclusiveness, as by reason of special celebration. These literary presentations are, in a particular sense, simple. Of course they are not simple to make; *that* they get made at all can be a matter of admiring astonishment. They are simple in the sense that to achieve the special celebration of something, they separate it out and give it exclusive attention.

Triumphant intelligibility, in the mode of special celebration, provides us with the heightened awareness of what something might be if it were free to develop its particular character. The imaginary garden, in this case, is highly exclusive; all those contrary influences that in actuality operate to menace, modify or curtail find no place in it. *Here* in *this* garden something can be what it might have been in the actual world if God or Nature had contrived the actual world for its special benefit, which is not the case.

When we greet the presentation of this particular concentrated "suchness" with the response: "Yes. That's exactly it!" we are drawing on our trans-literary experience
but not as an ordinary recognition of the familiar. What
operates here is the deep and, again, in no pejorative sense,
primitive awareness that everything *has* some particular
"suchness" that *would* shine forth in its concentrated essence if we could disengage it and see it with primordial
freshness of vision. This is how Adam saw the animals in
Paradise when they came before him for naming. Only
now you must imagine that there is just one elephant, one
butterfly, one swallow. How different each would seem to
be! The name for each must be especially invented and it
will not be a class-term, for the sense of emphatic, distinctive individuality makes the notion of classification fan-
tastically inappropriate. The imaginary garden in this
case is the local habitation and the name.

It will not be correct to say that this special celebration
is a falsification on the ground that things-in-the-world,
whether objects or psychic states, are not free and isolated
as they appear in the literary presentation. There remains
a sense in which, independent of all the influence of relationship, everything *has* its individual character. Who, in
actual experience, has not had a sudden conviction of this?
It is a sense of "a just thisness," and the awareness of it is
often associated with the feeling that if only we could keep
our attention on it, if only we could stay with it, if only we
could avoid distraction, it would display itself to us even
more completely than it now does. This "it" could be anything—a flower or a feeling. "Oh! if only I could arrest time
and process, the restless ongoing happening of the world,
the inevitable fluctuations of attention, I could perhaps
distill the concentrated pure essence of, for example, this
psychic state. Why must it go from me before I have fully
seen it?" The awareness of all this is deep in our experience; it lies just as deep as our sense of the life-chimera and

it should not be surprising that we greet as a case of triumphant intelligibility the literary presentation that, in its concentrated attention and special celebration, fending off all distraction, provides us with the possibility of "fully seeing."

Tennyson's song which begins "Now sleeps the crimson petal, now the white;" celebrates a pure romanticism protected from the encroachment of anything alien. Hopkins' sonnet which begins "No worst, there is none" radically different in tone and subject as it is, also centers in a pure concentrated essence. This terrible despair fills the world; there is nothing else. Our admiration for complex works of literary art in the mode of dramatic tension need not, and, in fact, does not interfere with our appreciation of these different literary achievements dedicated to the enterprise of special celebration.

There is a further, and still different, kind of triumphant intelligibility in literature. This is the luminous intelligibility of some structured hierarchical order. It might be called the intelligibility of symbolic reference. But "symbolic reference" as here employed, does not extend to everything that might be recognized as literary symbol, for it is one thing to use a symbol as a unit of meaning in a work of literature, and rather another to elevate symbolic correspondence into the main pattern of a total literary structure. If I may employ "symbolic reference" to refer to this latter, it can be said that allegory is the most clear and evident example of literary intelligibility in this mode. This is not to say it is the only, the most ambitious, or, to modern minds, the most acceptable manifestation. There is now a preference for the subtlety of sunken myth exercising from the depths its control over the literary presentation.

What I seek to designate here is a general pattern of intelligible structure which, in specific literary execution, is displayed with considerable variety. The difference between Dante's *Divine Comedy* and Thomas Mann's *The Magic Mountain* is manifest. Yet they have in common an emphasis on vertical order. By some system of symbolic reference, one level of being or of experience is related to another. Such works of literature, however informed by passion, have a kind of intellectuality. Their pattern of organization is animated by an inherent explanatory tendency. All explanation depends on the recognition of continuity and mediation, but the explanatory tendency reaches beyond this recognition. Everywhere it is fired by faith—faith in the prevalence of law. From this point of view an intelligible world is a lawful world. Law has its rigor, but this is not unacceptable. Indeed, the "air of reality" depends here on some impression of necessity.

There is a sense in which literature, in the mode of symbolic reference, though difficult to achieve in impressive form, is easiest to understand—not, that is, as an achievement but simply as an enterprise. This is because it has a certain resemblance to enterprises of explanation with which we are familiar in other quarters. Yet this very similarity can mislead us. All explanation involves generality, but the generality of literature is not like the generality of science, or of any theoretical scheme where the data constitute one thing and the explanatory account another, so that each admits of independent scrutiny. A work of literature is so constructed that it deliberately and intentionally blocks all attempts at such independent scrutiny. It is exactly this feature of literature that arouses suspicion in minds accustomed to see the distinction between the evidence and the claim as the indispensable sign of intellectual responsibility in making claims. Yet the intelligibility of a work of literature in the mode of symbolic reference depends upon this apparently suspect feature.

It is evident that the symbols of literature are incarnated. They are at the extreme remove from the symbols of mathematics or symbolic logic. But we miss the

point if we think of this incarnation primarily as a peda-
gogical device in the form of easy lessons for minds that
cannot soar. More nearly, it is illumination for minds that
can radiate from a centre while yet remaining within that
centre. The intelligibility depends not simply upon a relationship of this with that, but on the maintenance, at
every point, of a free passage of ascent and descent. Every
work of literature in the symbolic mode is a Jacob's ladder
"pitched between Heaven and Charing Cross."

I have said that all forms of explanation involve the
recognition of continuity and mediation. Science makes
use of this feature of the world, but it is to literature that
we must look if we wish to see it luminously *displayed*. It
is the display that counts for the sense of triumphant intelligibility rather than any particular doctrine, theory, or
dogma that may be used for this display. The nonacceptance of a dogma implicit in such a work of literature
leaves us still profoundly impressed by the successful display of symbolic mediation, and this response is the result
of an appeal to something deeper than the mere intellectual interest in "a point of view."

The particular "suchness" of the individual thing or
occurrence, and the enigmatic recalcitrance of contingent fact, is not all that our deep and primordial experience
affords, for both of these are what they are against the background of continuity and mediation. The impressive importance of a special celebration depends not only on our
sense of the protection against oppositional tendencies
that the imaginary garden affords; this garden also affords
protection against the assimilating tendency of any hierarchical order that would reduce the individual thing to
emblematic status. Thus our appreciation of the special
celebration depends on some awareness, that needs to be
felt but that need not be formulated, of these exclusions.
Similarly, our sense of dramatic tension, of paradox, of
irony, of yes-and-no-ness, involves more than the recogni-

tion of a single world within which these oppositional tensions can occur; it involves some awareness of oppositional tension *itself* to the pattern of some mediating order, for it is only by contrast to an explanatory mediating order that anything *can* present itself as recalcitrant. This is why works of literary art predominantly ordered by the vertical structure of symbolic correspondences can be greeted as right and can show forth as triumphantly intelligible. What we know, on the basis of our trans-literary experience, and know in some deep primitive or primordial way, is not any particular doctrine or point of view that may be exploited for the construction of such a work of literary art; what we know is simply the *reality* of relationships of correspondences, of mediating order, in the world of our experience.

These modes of triumphant intelligibility in literature bear a close similarity to what some philosophers, concerned with the phenomenology of experience, have distinguished as basic categories. Perhaps the most relevant account is that provided by the American philosopher C. S. Peirce. Peirce, with admirable simplicity, christened the categories Firstness, Secondness, and Thirdness. Firstness is being independent of anything else. It is particular "suchness," and it is associated with the ideas of originality, spontaneity, freedom. Secondness is reaction in relation to another. It is the mode of being of existence and relates to fact. It is associated with the ideas of effort, constraint, opposition. Thirdness is mediation. It involves continuity in nature and symbolic reference in discourse. It is associated with the ideas of order, law, harmony, explanation. These categories are categories because they are universal. In every state of affairs, according to Peirce, there is an element of real spontaneity, an element of brute factual obduracy, and an element of law.

Of course I cannot claim the authority of Peirce for anything I have said about intelligibility in literature, but the similarity has at least the interest of an analogy. Developing the analogy, one could say that what I have called "special celebration" is a case of Firstness; "dramatic tension" is a case of Secondness; "symbolic reference" is a case of Thirdness. If there is any illumination provided by this analogy, the suggestion arises that the "correspondence" of literature to something beyond itself might best be sought at the deep categorical level, in something more basic than anything describable as formulated opinion.

Now I think there is *something* in all of this. Yet it is insufficient, and a consideration of why it is insufficient can be instructive. What makes the view suggestive and even, perhaps, in a fashion, right, is the very thing that will make it wrong if put forward as a solution to the problem of literature and knowledge, put forward, that is, as something that is supposed to conduct us to journey's end. I refer to the classification. The classification may be, in itself, plausible enough, and it need not be supposed that there is anything intrinsically improper in classifying works of art. This is something we do all the time and it can be helpful and illuminating. But it remains the case that what makes individual art works individual is precisely what eludes classification. This consideration raises the question: Can it be sufficient to find the revelatory disclosure of works of literary art in some sort of general ontological insight?

Every philosophical theory, whether the one here elaborated or any other about literary art as ontological disclosure, *every* theory that claims that works of literary art are cognitively illuminating because they "bring out" some *general* character of reality or of experience, *must* be insufficient. The reason for this is that every such theory is committed to the assumption that works of literary art are illuminating and revelatory in that they are, in some way, illustrative. Now it need not be denied that literary presentations might be thus illustrative, but no amount of emphasis on the basic and fundamental importance of what is thus illustrated can render irrelevant the embarrassing question: why do we need so many illustrations? Bluntly put, if the cognitive importance of literary art is considered to consist *exclusively* in some sort of ontological or metaphysical insight, why should not a few cases suffice for the quick mind, and a few more cases for the not so quick mind? What accounts for the multiplication of works of literature? Why do we need this? Why do we welcome it?

So long as we cling to the view that to speak of works of literary art as revelatory involves a commitment to some version of the correspondence theory of truth—involves, that is, the assumption that a literary presentation is revelatory because it "corresponds" to something—we shall not be able to escape the illustrative theory of literature. Every such theory, whether naive or sophisticated, is bound to be insufficient. It will be insufficient because it will fail to account for the value we place on the individual disclosures of individual literary presentations.

Theorists who stress the importance of individual art works *as* individual are, of course, not wanting. Usually, though, the recommendation to prize the individual work of literature for itself is associated with the further recommendation to give over this insistence on literature as revelatory. The importance of literature, we are told, is that it provides us with experience. Why should we wish to insist that it should also provide us with knowledge? If what we want is knowledge, we can look elsewhere. But to this suggestion there is, I think, a reply. In the first place, it is not so much that we insist on cognitive insight as that we seem to get it. In the second place, if it can be said that we can look elsewhere for knowledge, it can also be said that we can look elsewhere for experience. If it is silly to turn to literature for knowledge, why should it not be equally silly to turn to it for experience? If we *do* turn from life to literature for experience it must be that experience, as exhibited in literature, is somehow different. What, after all, do we mean by "experience"? There is more to be taken account of here than may seem, initially, to be the case.

VI

Experience

THERE is nothing novel about the view that literary art is in some way intimately concerned with human experience. Yet it is sometimes the case that a familiar view, just because it is familiar, fails to receive the detailed consideration it merits. What, exactly, does it mean to say that literature is concerned with human experience?

There is a meaning of "subject-matter" according to which we can say that the subject-matter of a work of literary art could be anything—the song of the blackbird or an elaborate theological doctrine. Subject-matter in this sense is usually contrasted with realized content, since several works of literature might be said to have the same subject-matter but each its individual realized content. Realized content expresses or exhibits the possible human import of some subject-matter, "brings it home," as it were, in terms of some human reference. If this is so, there is a second meaning of "subject-matter" according to which we can say that the general subject-matter of all literary art is human experience. As we know, it is both idle and impertinent to stipulate requirements with respect to what a literary artist should use as raw material for the making of a work of literature, since it is only the artist himself who can have a sense, a feeling, an intimation, of what is or is not promising, and what presents itself as promising to one writer may have no appeal for another. Yet we do, nevertheless, expect, indeed require, that the literary artist must exhibit the humanistic significance of whatever it is he deals with, for literary art is first, last, and always about man. But it is not about man in the informational sense. A work of literature can accommodate information, for it can accommodate almost anything. The inclusion, in a novel, of information, even elaborately detailed information, on whaling or on forestry, is not objectionable if it can be seen to have a functional role in the total literary presentation. Though information on man is likely to be less manageable than information on other matters, it too can find assimilation if it is evident that it is not there simply for its own sake. The reason for this requirement is not far to seek. Information may be as important as you please, but talent in creative art is not required for the transmission of information. When we look to literature for illumination and insight we presumably look for something that literature is distinctively equipped to provide.

If, then, we can say that, according to *one* meaning, the general subject-matter of literary art is human experience, it will be appropriate to consider what we mean by "experience," and it will be useful to begin our inquiry with an examination of the nature of experience as actual life experience. Experience as encountered in literature may be, in certain respects, distinguishably different from experience as undergone in life, but unless we have a clear notion of what we mean by experience in life we shall find it hard to understand what experience might be in literature. Thus, we must be content, for the time being, to look away from literature and consider life.

John Dewey in the third chapter of *Art as Experience* remarked that although philosophers talk a lot about experience they usually fail to take account of the notion of *an* experience. When someone says that he has had *an* experience he does not merely mean that he has had experience, for experience is something we have every conscious moment. *An* experience, by contrast to mere experience, "stands out" from the general flow of conscious awareness and presents itself as having some kind of unity. The reference to "when someone says" is intended to refer to ordinary talk, not technical discourse. If we take account of technical discourse we quickly recognize that we cannot rely on grammar to bring out the kind of singularity that Dewey wishes to emphasize. There are contexts in which the phrase "an experience" functions for classification, for example, "a visual experience," "an emotional experience." We can readily see that this is not all that is involved in the context of conversation when someone reports that he has had an experience. What then is "an experience" as understood in this context? The answer Dewey offers to this question seems to me to be unsatisfactory as a general account, however much it may be relevant to certain special cases.

It is certainly obvious that *an* experience must stand out from the general flow of experience. Now since any experience, as actual life experience, is something that occurs and that takes time, it seemed to Dewey that the way *an* experience could stand out and be individualized was by means of a temporal pattern. Accordingly, he specifies as the distinguishing trait of *an* experience a temporal pattern of "inception, development, and consummation." Well, certainly an experience might present itself as having such a pattern, but it seems not plausible to suppose that such a pattern is an invariable feature of everything that might be referred to as *an* experience. When someone says: "Yesterday I had a strange (or interesting or delightful) experience," we certainly take him to be referring to something that occurred during a time, but we do not take it for granted that his experience necessarily had the kind of sequential structure specified by Dewey. What

takes time to be experienced is not necessarily experienced
as temporal in the sense that what is most evident and arresting about it is a pattern of "inception, development,
and consummation." For example, an experience might be
a case of what we call "sudden illumination." "While I was
watering the flowers, putting on my coat . . . I suddenly
got the idea of how to solve such and such a problem."
Then, again, an experience may be one that seems non-
temporal. The aesthetic appreciation of some visual effect
in nature—the diffusion of moonlight through mist, the
panoramic expanse, is not usually, certainly not necessarily, remembered as *an* experience because of a clearly
marked pattern of inception, development, and consummation. This is not to deny the possibility of such a pattern.
We would not be surprised if a person's account of an experience was presented with emphasis on sequential happening, for, after all, an experience can be something in
the nature of an adventure, something that plays itself out
as drama. Since *an* experience does indeed stand out from
the general flow of experience, we may be tempted to say
that it is in some way "dramatic," but if we do we must
remember that "dramatic" as it functions in ordinary
conversation does not always mean "playing itself out as
drama"; it sometimes means no more than "startling" or
"arresting" or "unusual" as, for example, the experience
of visual or auditory hallucination.

It is indeed the case that when an experience is life experience it has some temporal reference. Someone may
speak of *the* experience of first seeing the sea or the high
mountains; he may emphasize as *an* experience the occasion when he first realized something. Anything long heard
about and *then* experienced, such as nightingale's song or
religious awe, will be remembered as tied to a specific temporal "then"—the occasion when the experience was had.
But this does not mean that the experience *itself* is marked
by temporal pattern. Moreover, we often speak of an ex-

perience, in the singular sense, without even this reference
to the episodic. An experience of grief occasioned by the
death of someone can be endured as a kind of haunting op-
pressive presence that characterizes or colors some pro-
tracted period of our existence, however much the surface
play of life may provide this or that incidental pleasure or
delight.

In discussing the nature of *an* experience, Dewey is intent on emphasizing the fact that *an* experience may be
said to have "aesthetic quality." Certainly when and if
an experience has a marked formal pattern of inception,
development, and consummation, the claim that it has aesthetic quality is plausible enough, for it is easy to recognize
the aesthetic appeal of such a pattern. We can, of course,
take Dewey's account as having reference exclusively to
certain particular cases, but if we do, we shall have to find
some other account that will do justice to the wider range
of reference to "an experience" that seems to characterize
ordinary talk. "I had an experience of intense frustration
on the occasion when . . ." is not a remark that seems
odd to us, but this is certainly not a case of *an* experience
in Dewey's celebrative sense.

Dewey is certainly right in his claim that *an* experience,
in the singular sense, is something different from mere experience, but wrong, I would say, in assuming that what individuates experience is some clearly marked temporal
pattern. I would suggest that what individuates an experience, what makes it stand out from the general flow of experience, is the duality of self-reflexive awareness. *An* experience, as life experience, is self-consciously recognized
by the experiencer as *his*. An experience is not just awareness; it is awareness of awareness. Animals, no doubt,
can be said to have experiences but only a being capable of
self-consciousness can be said to have "an experience."

It is important to notice that awareness of awareness
is not to be identified with every case of heightened aware-

ness. The close and concentrated focusing of attention on something—the exact color of the sodium flame, the exact rhythm of the patient's heart beat—provides a heightened awareness of what is scrutinized, but if no evident sense of *being* aware is here included, no self-reference, then this is not awareness of awareness and therefore not a case of an experience in the singular sense. Of course there is an object of attention in cases of awareness of awareness and it need not be thought that the object here is some pure psychic occurrence, some pure mental act. It may be doubted whether we can catch such a thing, and, in any case, the self involved in "an experience" is not some mysterious pure ego but a particular person. An awareness of awareness is *both* an awareness of something given in experience, *and also* an awareness of a mode or manner of experiencing it, in short, it is a "me-experiencing-this." How much emphasis there may be on "me" and how much on "this" will vary from occasion to occasion.

Every kind of awareness of awareness involves a duality of the self—the self who is aware and the self who is aware of being aware—but how sharply these selves are distinguished will depend on the nature of the experience and the circumstance of its occurrence. An experience can be such as to involve only a minimal distinction in the form of awareness of response. There is something experienced with a response of delight, or distress, or surprise. There must, of course, be a self who is aware of the responding "me," but this self may not show forth as sharply distinguished on every occasion. I can be aware of how I am "taking," of how I am responding to, or undergoing, some presented something without a pronounced sense of separation between the responding "me" and the apprehending "I." But this duality of the "me" and the "I" which is implicitly operative can show forth as sharply marked. These are the occasions when the responding "me" is observed as from a distance, that is, apprehended as a phenomenal self who plays a role in a situation. The responding self and the observing self can be so separated that the observing self watches with wonder, or pleased surprise, or helpless distress, the role enacted by the phenomenal self. This sense of separation, of duality of the self, is most clearly marked when the response of the observing self is a response to the response of the observed self and any such state of affairs necessarily presupposes a still further self who is aware of the response of the observing self. If this talk of a self behind the self behind the self sounds queer, I can only plead that the queerness, after all, resides in us.

Every form of self-conscious awareness, every case of awareness of awareness involves the assumption of an elusive, "ungetatable," observing self. If we try to observe this observing self, questioning, for example, whether its observation is biased or impartial, we can do this only by retreating to a further self. It is useless to be exasperated or tantalized by this state of affairs and it is unnecessary to construe it as a situation that makes knowledge impossible. Knowledge always involves some distinction between the knower and what is known; to be unhappy with this distinction and to hanker for some sort of transcendent identity is no doubt to hanker for something but something necessarily noncognitive. There is, indeed, a difference between "knowing remotely" and "knowing intimately," but we delude ourselves if we suppose that the advantages that accrue to intimate knowing can be carried further and further until we find a consummation in identification. The elimination of all duality is the elimination of knowledge. This is because *to know* is one thing and *to be* is another.

No person exists who has not had "an experience"; indeed we have all had many such, but a little reflection is sufficient to suggest that persons may differ considerably in the interest they take in this state of affairs. Broadly and generally speaking, what degree of understanding we have with regard to anything depends only partly on native intelligence; it depends mostly on interest. Subtlety of perception, delicacy of discernment, are largely a matter of cultivation, and cultivation is dependent on interest. It is, then, to be expected that persons will differ in the degree to which they take account of the distinctive character of their experience, and this is to say that awareness of awareness can vary from little more than simple recognition to relatively full realization.

It will be important, in this connection, to consider the meaning of the word "realize." There is a perfectly intelligible meaning of "realize" which is synonymous with "recognize" as used in such queries as: "Do you realize the causal connection between X and Y?" "Do you realize the practical advantage of going about the task this way?" In all such cases "recognize" can be substituted for "realize" without any distortion of meaning. But there are cases when "realize" is differently used, cases where we concede recognition but look for or require something more. It could happen that when someone says that he realizes the difficulty of my situation, I might think to myself: "He doesn't realize a thing! He doesn't realize it at all! He merely recognizes that it is the kind of situation that might be called difficult." When we hear the note of urgent requirement in such imperatives as: "Realize how he must feel!" "Realize how the situation must appear to him!" we are aware of being called upon to do something more than merely recognize the existence of some state of affairs. This difference is not quite adequately understood if we interpret it as the difference between thought and feeling, intellect and emotion, for though we may be asked to realize a feeling or emotional state, we can, with equal propriety, be asked to realize a conviction or belief. The essential thing, in either case, is to apprehend it *as* a form or mode of human experience. To realize our own experience is to attend to the qualitative character of our mode of having or undergoing it; to realize another person's experience is to engage in an act of imaginative participation. So much for actual life experience. Let us now consider literary experience.

What is it that we experience when we read a poem or other work of literary art? It seems that what we experience is itself experience. The experience expressed, articulated, formalized, or, one might say, incarnated, in the poem, is the object of our apprehension when we read the poem and our experience of the poem is an experience of this experience. Thus the phrase "literary experience" is ambiguous, since experience may be qualified as literary because it is experience raised to the level of literary expression, or because it is experience derived from literature, as distinguished from that derived from life. Literary experience, in the latter sense, is actual experience, for it is always someone's experience, but literary experience in the former sense is not actual experience. Caught out of the flux of nature, it is not evanescent, not a perishing occurrence; it is permanent and stable. Accordingly, "realization" as the enterprise of the literary artist is not identical with "realization" as the task of the reader; the former is creative articulation, the latter is imaginative apprehension. But in so far as a reader succeeds with a work of literature with which the artist has succeeded, what the reader apprehends can properly be said to be a realization of a realization.

We take it for granted that a good reader will, in initial encounter, expose himself with a completely open, free, and unguarded receptivity to the deliverance of the poem. Critical analysis and all that goes with it is a perfectly appropriate activity, but it is appropriate only as an activity subsequent to the hospitality of an unguarded reception. It will be characteristic of any such initial reception, if it moves unimpeded and is not forced into self-consciousness by the distress of noncomprehension, that what we experience will seem to be the very experience that is the poem.

It is after the event that we remember what we know, namely, that there can be a difference between the experience presented in the poem and our experience of it, since, with respect to that to which we respond, our experience can be in many ways incomplete or incorrect. It is the recognition of this that leads to analysis and deliberate intellectual scrutiny. All such analysis is, of course, based on the belief that postanalytical apprehension can be superior to preanalytical encounter. Yet this belief is not incompatible with a concern for the innocence of initial reception which derives from the recognition that feeling can be prior to formulation and that we can sense such a thing as power and presence before we can say, much less explain, wherein it lies. I am here distinguishing between ignorance and innocence. Ignorance is a fact of nature; innocence is a spiritual discipline achieved by intent, and this discipline is for the nonignorant, the reader who has a wide knowledge of other works of literature. In the end, of course, the understanding of any work of literature must depend heavily on the appropriate use of just this knowledge; the discipline of innocence in initial reception is a matter of courage and confidence, comparable to the noble gesture ascribed to the Bedouin Arab who first extends hospitality to the stranger and only afterwards inquires about his identity and business.

As I have already noted, the experience of the reader can in one sense be called "literary" in that it is an experience derived from literature. We may wish to distinguish such experience from "ordinary" experience, the experience that accrues when we put down the book and take up the tasks and adventures of life, and we sometimes make the distinction by referring to literary experience as contemplative or imaginative. But it is to be observed that contemplating or imagining, however little it may show as gross overt behavior is, none the less, activity. It uses up time, it uses up energy, and it can be engaged in with various degrees of concentration and proficiency. Consequently, this, whatever its peculiarity, is actual experience. But the experience incarnated in the poem, the experience that is the very substance of the poem, is not actual experience. It cannot be said to be the poet's experience, since the poet is a person and any experience of a person is a perishing occurrence. It is not fully satisfactory to speak of it as a record of the poet's experience because any such way of talk is likely to introduce the question: How accurate? How reliable? and we are not concerned with this. It is perhaps best to adopt the phrase suggested by Susanne Langer in *Feeling and Form* and speak of it as "virtual experience."

We need not suppose that every work of literary art is "a monument of unaging intellect" or that even the best are absolutely immune from the tooth of time; nevertheless, the contrast between the passing and perishing character of actual experience and the enduring fixity of non-occurrent virtual experience is sufficiently impressive. The virtual experience presented in literary art is far more available for realization than actual life experience. It is not simply that it will "stand still to be examined," that it can be reapprehended by the reader. As something "made," rather than merely "found," it can be not only shaped and formed by the literary artist, but elaborated and developed in point of subtlety and in point of complexity. It is therefore hardly a matter for wonder that we should look to literary art for a disclosure of the possibilities of experience, for an understanding of what things might come to *as* forms or modes of human experience. Yet the understanding of literature and the appreciation of its superior luminosity would not be possible if life experience provided no occasion for realization. If I am correct in my account of "an experience" as somebody's life experience, "having an experience" involves at least some degree of realization, a realization not only of something given or occurrent but of "what it is like" to apprehend this given, to undergo this happening. The chief, though by no means the only, difference between realizations achieved in life and realizations provided by literary art is that the latter can be superior in point of elaboration and in point of intelligibility.

It may be helpful, at this stage, to gather up some conclusions. There certainly is a difference between experience, considered as just any kind or form of conscious awareness, and what, in ordinary conversation, would be referred to as "an experience." An experience, in the singular sense, might happen to have the temporal pattern of "inception, development, consummation" emphasized by Dewey, but this is not an invariable feature of everything that might be referred to as "an experience." What *is* an invariable feature is the presence of some kind of duality; there is something experienced together with some awareness of *how* what is experienced *is* experienced. This is why "an experience" is not just awareness but awareness of awareness. Although every case of "an experience" as life experience involves this duality, and therefore involves some degree of what we can call "realization," the extent of such realization can vary from person to person, and from occasion to occasion.

Experience, as embodied in literary art, is not actual experience. It may be derived from actual experience, but it is not itself actual experience; it is more properly referred to as virtual experience. This virtual experience, embodied, objectified, expressed, in the literary presentation has a kind of "public presence" and a kind of "permanent presence" not possible in any case of actual experience. Because it has a public presence it is potentially sharable, and because it has a permanent presence it is more available for full realization than actual experience can be. For these reasons, it may not seem surprising that we should look to literary art for the better understanding of the possibilities of experience.

But the question that must now be considered is this: Will it be appropriate to regard the kind of realization that is involved in "an experience" as a case of knowledge? There are theorists, particularly philosophical theorists, who wish to contrast what they would call "experience" with what they would call "knowledge." Experience, they tell us, is just experience. Of course experience involves awareness, but there is no good reason to suppose that mere awareness is the same thing as knowledge. I agree that there is, indeed, no good reason. However, if I am correct in my view that what is singled out as "an experience" is never just a case of mere awareness but always a matter of awareness of awareness, the question of the use of the term "knowledge" with reference to this remains open for consideration.

VII

Understanding as Realization

THE question: What is knowledge? is ancient and persistent in philosophical inquiry, but since knowledge is not something that can be found, in the sense in which gold can be found, the question is really of the form: What shall be called knowledge? Because knowledge is thought of as something desired and sought, and because it is assumed that the possession of knowledge is a good thing, "knowledge" will not function as a purely descriptive term, that is to say, it will be to some extent normative or evaluative. Consequently, we should not be surprised to encounter differences of opinion on what should be called knowledge and linguistic recommendations, implicit or explicit, on this matter. For example, Descartes' *Meditations* opens with the troubled question of whether he really knows anything. From the common sense point of view this is preposterous, for here is a man of mature years who has had an extensive education and a wide experience of the world. But it rapidly becomes evident that what Descartes means by "knowledge" is indubitable knowledge, so that his question is, in effect: Can I be said to know anything beyond the peradventure of a doubt?

Not all philosophers are concerned with what has been called "the quest for certainty," but the association of knowledge with quest is broadly operative in philosophy, so that modern analytical or linguistic philosophers who are concerned not so much with seeking knowledge in the sense in which Descartes sought it, as with clarifying the concept of knowledge, elucidating the meaning of "knowledge" or of "know," will still tend to think of knowledge as something sought, something that may be achieved or missed. Accordingly, "I know" or "he knows" will present itself as a claim that naturally and quickly suggests the propriety of the request for evidence. This tendency has perhaps been further enforced by the influence of the philosophical movement known as logical positivism, but I think that, quite apart from this influence, the whole contentious character of philosophy, its association with argument, with debate, with objections, and replies to objections, has the accumulative effect of endowing the word "know" with a certain powerful psychic charge. By this I mean that the word "know" is not just a word, it is a word that instantly alerts attention in philosophers and quickly evokes the question: How do you know? Since, then, "knowledge" and "know" are words of weight, we must expect to encounter stipulative requirements about their use, but whereas earlier philosophers would be likely to reject a suggestion that something was knowlege by saying that it was not really knowledge, not truly knowledge, not knowledge in the full sense or in the real right sense, modern philosophers are more likely to reject a suggestion by saying: "It would be misleading to call that knowledge."

It is worth noticing that the philosophical complaint that a form of language is misleading is a product of two judgments. There is first the judgment that the language leads in a certain direction, and there is then the judgment that in so leading it misleads because what it leads to is wrong, unwarranted, irresponsible, or in *some* way objectionable. Now, whereas the first judgment—this linguistic expression leads in such and such a direction—is arrived at by tracing out what the language implies or suggests, and this, we may say, is pure linguistic analysis, yet the second judgment—that in so leading it misleads—carries us beyond this.

The settled desire on the part of many modern philosophers to associate the primary meaning of "know" with claim, and to associate claim with the logical propriety of the request for evidence, springs from a concern not so much for certainty as for responsibility, that is to say, the concern is basically a moral concern. Now a moral concern is a proper concern, and it can and should elicit serious and sympathetic consideration. It does not seem odd to say that there can be responsible and irresponsible uses of "know" or claims to knowledge, and to believe that the difference is a matter of considerable importance, that, in the end, nothing less than the liberty and felicity of mankind may be here at stake. I am aware that to present the issue this way is somewhat to overstate the case but it is better, I think, that the case be overstated than overlooked. The point of bringing out the issue of concern is not to disallow the propriety of such a concern, but to make it possible to raise the question of whether this concern is *always* relevant.

There is nothing whatever objectionable about an explicit linguistic recommendation of the form: Let us confine the employment of the word "know" to such and such cases. But a recommendation must always be supported by reasons, for we cannot be expected to adopt it without reasons. It would certainly seem that an ultimate reason having reference to the liberty and felicity of mankind is a very powerful reason, but then something must be produced to persuade us that the rejection of the recommendation does indeed constitute "a clear and present danger." Unfortunately it is often the case that what is, in point of fact, a recommendation *for* use is presented in philosophic discourse as analysis of meaning *in* use. Such procedure should not be attributed to duplicity on the part of philosophers. A vigorous and lively conviction that only certain employments of the word "know" are responsible employments easily passes over into the belief that these are the only intelligible employments. "If you will reflect, you must see that you can't be meaning anything else." But we may ask: Is it unintelligible or improper to mean anything else, and if it is improper, just why is it improper?

A philosophical analysis of the meaning of "know" that is at present widely influential is one that finds two fundamental and irreducible meanings in use. There is knowing in the sense of *knowing that* (such and such is so), and there is knowing in the sense of *knowing how* (to perform some act). The delineation of these differences in meaning is lucidly presented in Gilbert Ryle's *The Concept of Mind*. It requires only a little reflection to see what there is about these employments of "knowing" that makes them particularly acceptable in some philosophical quarters. Both of them associate the use of "know" with claim, and claim with the appropriateness of request for evidence. If I say that I know that such and such is so, the request for evidence seems appropriate, however much, in some situations, it may be tiresome or unnecessary to insist upon it. Similarly, if I say that I know how to carry out some activity, such as swim or speak French, it is always logically appropriate to request that the claim be backed by performance. In short, these employments of "know" are seen as responsible. It is a quick but crucial step to move from "these are the only acceptable and responsible meanings" to "these are the only intelligible meanings." Of course, what a philosopher finds unacceptable he will easily find unintelligible, but if "unintelligible" is supposed to mean unintelligible in the context of ordinary talk on the part of persons who understand and use the English language, it has to be said that, in point of linguistic fact, these selected and endorsed meanings are not the only meanings.

It will, indeed, be generally recognized that there is a common use of "know" followed by the direct object, as in "I know Boston," "I know the color scarlet." Bertrand Russell suggested that we might use the phrase "knowledge by acquaintance" to bring out the English meaning of "to know" that corresponds to the French "connaître" or to the German "kennen." However, the philosophical use that Russell made of the phrase "knowledge by acquaintance" turned out to be much more restricted. In any case, modern philosophers, preoccupied with the concern for responsibility, will not hesitate to pronounce the phrase "knowledge by acquaintance" to be misleading. It suggests a way of knowing which, as direct, could not be subject to error. Of course, on the basis of acquaintance with something one might derive knowledge about that thing, but any form of knowledge about something is stateable in the claim that such and such is so. Also, any statement of the form "I know Boston" can be transposed into "I am acquainted with Boston," and this, in turn, can be interpreted to mean "there has been at least one event of encounter between me and Boston." The point of such interpretation being, of course, that in theory, if not always in practice, evidence for the occurrence of an event can be secured. Now, if to this it be protested: "But surely acquaintance provides something one just would not have without the acquaintance," the answer is likely to be: "Yes, indeed. But don't call that something knowledge; call it awareness." Does it matter what things are called? Yes. It does. We simply delude ourselves if we try to pretend that it does not. "Knowledge" can be seen as a dangerous word, a word that may do damage unless it is carefully and responsibly used. "Awareness," by contrast, is innocent. It does not seem to have mischief-making potentiality.

But however much we may understand sympathetically the point of view of philosophers preoccupied with

the concern for responsibility, it is still appropriate to
consider whether the stipulative requirements associated
with this concern might not have the effect of imposing
upon certain ordinary ways of talk an interpretation that
deprives them of their meaning. If we should have reason
to suppose that this is the case, there is the further question of whether we stand to lose something by the neglect
of this meaning.

There is a character, a *dramatis persona,* often in-
voked by philosophers in their argumentative struggle
with other philosophers. This *dramatis persona* is called
"the plain man." Philosophers have been known to cry
out against other philosophers: "Well, at any rate, I have
the plain man on my side." The reader may wonder why
a philosopher should think it important to have the plain
man, who in this context is the nonphilosopher, on his
side. After all, scientists do not care a bit about the opinion of nonscientists. But the philosopher is not in the position of the scientist. Since he carries out no experimental
inquiry, he has to deal with the data of ordinary experience, and although he tries to arrive at views that are more
systematic and lucid than the unreflective views of common sense, he is often a bit concerned about getting too
far away from common sense. To be sure not all philosophers have felt this scruple; in the history of philosophic
speculation we encounter a number of philosophers, beginning perhaps with "our father Parmenides" as Plato
called him, who have had little concern with the opinion
of the plain man. Yet the tendency to evoke the plain man
and to claim his support is a fairly common philosophic
gambit. But the odd thing about this is that philosophers
can dispute as to which has the plain man on his side without ever trying to settle the matter by directly asking the
plain man. In Berkeley's *Dialogues Between Hylas and
Philonous,* there is a point where Philonous says: "Ask
the gardener yonder." Philonous then proceeds to report

what, if asked, the gardener would reply, and this, naturally enough, is what Philonous would say. But Hylas is not persuaded. He thinks he knows the real opinion of the gardener and this, not so oddly, turns out to be Hylas's view. Well, of course, Hylas and Philonous are fictitious philosophers, but actual philosophers have debated in like manner without it ever occurring to them to "ask the gardener."

It would seem that nothing is so easy as to ask the plain man. Find a man. Ascertain that he is not a philosopher and has had no commerce with philosophy. There you have uncorrupted innocence. Ask him. But there is a difficulty about this; the difficulty is that by the time the question has been formulated clearly enough for debate, the issue has been put in such terms that the plain man will not understand it, or, at any rate, will not understand its implications. Thus asking the plain man will not result in the decisive and helpful "Yes" or "No" but in the puzzled query: "What do you mean?" Yet if we proceed to the explanation of what we mean, we are, to that extent, subjecting the man to philosophy and so destroying his innocence—the very innocence to which he owes his status as uncontaminated plain man.

However, though we are debarred from providing direct evidence to back the claim that we have the plain man on our side, it is possible to furnish something in the way of indirect evidence. This consists in inventing some account of an ordinary situation in which ordinary talk goes on and showing that some philosophical decision on permissible meaning distorts what would otherwise pass as ordinary meaning. The kind of talk I wish to consider is talk about individualized experiences and about knowing what they are like. Examples of such talk would be: "I know what it's like to be lost in a forest at night," "I know what it's like suddenly and unexpectedly to fall in love," "I know what it's like to be shipwrecked at sea," "I know what it's like to undergo religious conversion," "I know what it's like to tremble on the verge of madness" and so on. There can be no serious doubt about the occurrence of such talk, the question is: How are we to take it? How are we to interpret it?

Let us imagine a situation in which there are a number of plain men and one philosopher. This philosopher, henceforth simply referred to as the philosopher, is one who is determined not to countenance the claim "I know" unless this claim is associated with the propriety of the request for evidence. A plain man speaks up and says: "Oh I know what it's like to be poor and lonely in a big city." The other plain men accept this at face value, for, after all, this sort of remark is fairly common. But the philosopher turns to the speaker and says "Well, if you know what it is like, report on what it is like." The man so addressed begins with his report but he breaks off fairly soon and says: "I'm sorry, I can't explain very well." The other plain men accept this also. They do not find it odd to suppose that there might be knowing beyond saying. Not so the philosopher. He turns to the man and says: "If you don't know that the experience is such and such and so and so, and you don't know how to perform the act of reporting on it, then you just don't know." To this the plain man responds with some show of indignation. "But I *do* know, I tell you I *have* been poor and lonely in a big city, I've *undergone* it, I've *experienced* it!" To this the philosopher replies: "Oh my dear fellow, I don't doubt *that.* Your having been poor and lonely in a big city is an event of your biography. Evidence for the occurrence of this event is, no doubt, capable of being secured, but, I assure you, I'm quite willing to take your word for it." The response of the plain man to this is bafflement. The philosopher's way of talk is odd because among plain men using the English language as it is ordinarily used, it is taken for granted that if a man has undergone what we call "an experience," he knows what it is like simply and solely on the basis of his having had the experience.

This knowing is not the acquisition of information, or of inferential knowledge about something, as I might know that the cat is in the house on the basis of acquaintance with the cat-in-house situation, it is knowing in the sense of realizing by living through. If I say: "I know what an experience of having a visual hallucination is like, I've had one," the language I use asserts a claim: "I know what it's like" and backs this claim with "I've had one." This, at any rate, is how the remark would ordinarily be understood. Well, then, since here is claim *and* evidence, why should our philosopher be uneasy with it? The reason is that the preoccupation with the issue of responsibility leads to the view that nothing should be called evidence unless it is public and checkable evidence. Consequently what, in ordinary discourse, would be taken as evidence is seen as not the kind of thing that should be called evidence. This is not what "evidence" means in the context of scientific discourse, and indeed, this is not what "evidence" means in the context of argument. If we take account of the influence on philosophers of such paradigm models, we shall understand the wish to construe "I know what it's like, I've experienced it" not as performing the dual function of asserting and backing a claim, but as a linguistic statement that makes *two* claims for each of which independent evidence must be furnished. Evidence for "I know what it's like" must be report about the characteristics of the experience. Evidence for "I've experienced it" must be evidence for the event of encounter. This interpretation distorts ordinary meaning, and will, for this reason, seem odd and baffling.

Supposing one should try to rescue ordinary meaning by saying: "But look here, surely encounter does provide a kind of knowing that one just wouldn't have without the encounter" the philosopher has another resource for dealing with this. He may say: "Well, all right, there *is* a recognized meaning of 'know' followed by the direct object. It is quite proper for a person to say that he knows the color scarlet. This asserts the event of encounter and, assuming this event, we can take it that the event has engendered an awareness, namely, awareness of scarlet. Now, in the same way we can acknowledge awareness of lost-in-a-forest-at-night situation, or poor-and-lonely-in-a-big city situation, but surely there is no reason to speak of mere awareness as knowledge." This statement, however, presupposes that every transition from awareness to what may be called knowledge is a matter of inference, and this assumption can be challenged.

There is a difference between experiencing in the sense of living through, and experiencing in the simple sense of being aware of. Let us consider, in this connection, the difference between experience of pain and experience of color. From the view of scientific psychology awareness of pain and awareness of color are both regarded as cases of sensory response. Given the scientific point of view, this is perfectly proper because whether or not something is to be classified as a sensation is not at all a matter of how it is experienced; it is entirely a matter of whether we can specify a sense organ, such as free nerve endings. However, if we turn to the consideration of *how things are experienced*—the phenomenology of experience—the situation is different. Pain is experienced as phenomenally subjective; it is "in me." Color is experienced as phenomenally objective; it is "out there." This is why, if we trust simply to the deliverance of experience, putting aside any beliefs we may entertain as a consequence of scientific inquiry, it seems perfectly plausible to say: There may certainly be unseen colors but there cannot be unfelt pains. Consequently, when I am in pain, if I am in no doubt about the pain, I am equally in no doubt that it is *my* pain. Thus, I know more than that I am in pain, I know more than the pain, I know what it is like for me to suffer this pain.

The question: How do you know you are in pain? is not a sensible question if it is a question that asks for evidence, but the question: How do you know? need not be interpreted as a question concerning evidence. It can be understood as a question about manner of knowing. So interpreted, the question has an answer, and the answer, I believe, is: I know I am in pain by living through the pain experience. *An* experience is not just experience, it is lived experience, and every case of lived experience affords some degree of realization.

It is certainly evident that my knowing that I am in pain is not a matter of inference from observation, but, because of the I-me duality, implicit in every case of *an* experience, there is a sense in which we can speak of observing or witnessing. Consider the remark: "I observed with satisfaction that I was enduring the pain with composure." There is the suffering self which, as suffering, is not in a state of satisfaction, but there can be a witnessing self who responds with satisfaction to the way the suffering self is enduring its suffering. In short, experiencing, in the sense of living through, is not to be identified with any simple situation of mere awareness.

The notion of knowing by living through, and the belief that there is a kind of understanding to be achieved by this means, will not, I think, strike the ordinary person as in any way odd. We have all heard the remark: "Oh if only you could experience it, or something like it, you would understand!" *Recognizing* that such and such is so with reference to some kind of human experience is not the same thing as *realizing* what this might be like as lived experience. Confession of failure to understand, in the sense of realize, is perfectly compatible with absence of doubt concerning matter-of-fact. For example, "I do not doubt that certain persons enjoy situations of physical danger and even seek them out, but I don't understand it." What the speaker does not understand is the lure, the fascination, of danger. Again, to know that men have believed in demonic possession is not the same thing as entering imaginatively into the experience of entertaining this belief. If we distinguish, as we should, between the tenability of a belief and the experience of entertaining the belief, or the experience generated by that entertainment, we will be ready to acknowledge that anything that might assist us to an imaginative participation can properly be said to extend the range of our humanistic understanding.

When someone says, with reference to some kind of human experience, "I know what it's like. I've lived through it. I've experienced it," we commonly accept that he does know, even when he cannot convey this knowledge. Knowing beyond saying is acceptable in such a case, not because saying is impossible, but because the only kind of saying that would be relevant is a saying that requires some degree of literary talent. Mere fluency in the language is adequate for informational report, but talent is necessary for the imaginative evocation of vicarious experience. This brings us back to the consideration of literary art.

Life is one thing and literature is another. No sensible person supposes that literature is a substitute for life, for there is much to life that transcends the interest in understanding. It is in reference to this interest that literature is superior to life. The reasons are not far to seek, and they can be brought out by considering the contrast between virtual experience as presented in works of literary art, and actual experience as undergone in the process of living.

Actual experience must be some particular person's actual experience and it has the idiosyncratic character of life in the sense of "a life," your life, my life. An experience, as actual experience, is usually an episode in some individual's life. The descriptive phrases we use to refer to cases of an experience have a generality that tends to disguise the degree of individual variation that in fact prevails. We rather too hastily say: "I know just what your experience must have been, I too have (fallen suddenly in love, lost a child by death, and so on)." We tend to refer to *the* experience of being poor and lonely in a big city, but a little reflection tells us that what this experience may have been depends on a wide variety of factors, such as previous experience, duration, age, sex, temperament and the rest. We know something, to be sure, but how much is another matter. By contrast to the personal and idiosyncratic character of actual experience, virtual experience as presented in works of literary art is not any particular person's experience; it is therefore available *for* any person to experience, that is to say, virtual experience is potentially shareable as actual experience cannot be.

Then, again, virtual experience as objectified and embodied in literature will "stand still" to be re-experienced. It can be considered, discussed, and it presents itself as subject for critical elucidation. By contrast, anything to be realized in actual experience must be realized in passage, caught on the wing, so to speak. Actual experience just "happens"; virtual experience is "made." Because virtual experience is made, it can be shaped, formed, complicated and elaborated far beyond the range of anything that could be provided in actual experience. By way of example we may consider the extent to which highly complicated ideational material ("ideas") can find accommodation in literary art. Referring to actual experience, we would not be likely to speak of the experience of entertaining highly complicated beliefs, doctrines, "points of view." Actual experience is too idiosyncratic, too accidental, too fragmentary, to allow for this. If we wish to realize most fully what the entertainment of belief might come to we must turn to literature. It is correct, I think, to say that what counts in literary art is not doctrine, simply as such, but the entertainment of doctrine. Nevertheless the elaboration of what each entertainment might come to as a form of human experience provides an illumination, a kind of understanding, that no amount of strict logical analysis of doctrine can provide.

Virtual experience could not be what it is if it were mere report, even evocative report, of actual experience. No doubt part of the talent of the talented literary artist consists in his more than usual perceptiveness and his more than usual capacity to apprehend the possibilities latent in actual experience. Henry James, commenting on the common advice offered to aspiring authors, "write out of your experience," adds "but be sure you are the kind of person on whom no experience is lost." Experience is "lost" to the extent that its nature and its implicit potentialities are not realized. Yet this, important as it is, is only half the story. The talent of the talented artist is linguistic, and, for the literary artist, language is not a vehicle for report but a creative and transforming power. In short, literary art is made out of the resources of experience and out of the resources of language. We could, perhaps, say, as a very rough generalization, that the novelist counts somewhat more on the exploitation of experience, and the poet somewhat more on the expoitation of language, but since both must count on both, this can only be a matter of degree and of emphasis.

It is proper enough to say that the poet counts on the suggestions of language, that his commerce with words is not adequately described as the search for the right words that will fit an already fully determinate something. That something is not fully determinate, not fully in being, until it has been given its formed and structured habitation and its Proper Name. All the same, there is that something

that clamors for habitation and name and that something
has its own recalcitrance. It will not be forced into *any*
habitation, it will not accept *any* name. Word-play is useful exericse for the aspiring poet. "Move words around and
listen to how they sound and what they say, catch the tone
and swing of rhythms and notice their formative influence." This is salutary advice, and it is far better to offer
this advice than to mutter something vague about "writing from the heart." But however useful exercises may
be for art, exercises are not yet art. The poet knows as well
as anyone that technique is for use and that he must, in
the end, have something to say. In *Making, Knowing and
Judging,* W. H. Auden remarks: "He will never know
what he himself *can write* until he has a general sense of
what *needs to be written.*" The fact that the poet must
find his own subject does not mean that he can dispense
with this finding or that this subject, when found, does not
impose on the poet its own challenging demands.

The poet, or other literary artist, seeks to know in the
sense of to realize. He differs from the rest of us in that
he is commonly far more exacting with respect to what he
will count as realization, and he is commonly far more ambitious with respect to what he seeks to realize. Were it
not for the testimony of literary art, those of us who are not
literary artists would never suppose, dream or imagine
that the kind of complicated material that finds expression
in literature was ever available *for* realization.

I have sought to defend the cogency of the common remark: "You don't really know what it is unless and until
you've experienced it." Of course, this remark has its own
biased emphasis. Knowledge in the sense of knowledge
about something, *is* knowledge and *really* knowledge. For
many purposes knowledge about is the kind of knowledge
we need. This is so evident, so obvious, that any attempt to
defend this notion of knowledge would seem gratuitous
in the extreme. So little is it in need of recognition that it

easily shows forth as the paradigm case of knowledge. Since all claims to knowing in the sense of knowing about something raise the issue of whether such claims are warranted or unwarranted and, therefore, the notions of truth and falsity, the question can be raised as to whether a plea for the recognition of knowledge in some different sense has any relevance to these notions. Is it appropriate to speak of truth in reference to literary art, and, if it is, what can we mean by "truth"?

VIII

Truth as Authenticity

"KNOWLEDGE" can be contrasted with "ignorance" and "knowledge" can be contrasted with "error." Any term that admits of two contrasts must be expected to operate somewhat differently in each association. When knowledge is contrasted with ignorance, rather than with error, it is a matter of degree and can vary from some minimum to relatively full knowledge. Accordingly, appraisal of knowledge is made by reference to degree. We ask: How full, how complete, how comprehensive? But when knowledge is contrasted with error, rather than with ignorance, the situation is different. In this case it does not seem to make intelligible sense to speak of "appraising knowledge" although, of course, we can have judgment about the utility of knowledge for some purpose. The reason for this is that, when knowledge is contrasted with error, knowledge is always correct or true, which, of course, is not to say that *knowledge-claims* are always correct or true.

A little reflection on this dual contrast of the word "knowledge" should suffice to tell us that if the question be asked: Is it the case that any use of the word "knowledge" logically involves some reference to truth? the answer must be that, if, when we speak of knowledge, we have in mind the contrast of knowledge with error, then certainly there is such a reference, but if we are thinking of knowledge as contrasted with ignorance, the situation is not so clear. Before we consider the possible relevance or irrelevance of the notion of truth in cases where knowledge is contrasted with ignorance, it will be necessary to discuss the contrast of knowledge with error.

When I say that I know that such and such is so, I am not so much reporting a state of affairs as voicing a claim. Whether this claim is warranted does not depend on how confident I feel. Knowledge-claims can be voiced with varying degrees of confidence. "I know that . . ." "I think that . . ." "I am, on the whole, inclined to believe that . . ." and so on. Degrees of confidence in voicing knowledge-claims may depend on the complexity of what is asserted, but they may also reflect difference in temperament or difference in training on the part of the speaker. Since there is always a distinction between the psychological fact *that* I think or believe such and such, and *what* I think or believe, knowledge-claims voiced with unhesitating confidence may be false and knowledge-claims voiced with hesitant caution may be true. But however such claims are voiced they are claims, in the particular sense of claims to knowledge about, and this accounts for a requirement in the use of "know" as it functions in this context. If I say that I think or believe that such and such is so, and later say that I now recognize that this is not the case, the circumstance that I no longer think or believe it leaves untouched the fact that I did once so think or believe. But if I say that I know that such and such is so, and later retract this claim, it is generally considered that I must retract not only the "that such and such is so" but also the justification or propriety of the earlier use of the word "know." I am expected to say something like: "I thought I knew but evidently I didn't." "I once knew it but I now don't," does not function analogously to "I once believed it but I now don't"; it has a

different meaning, referring to the contrast between re-
tention and forgetfulness, as in: "I once knew his date of
birth but I now don't." Thus, whereas it is quite possible
to think or believe what is not the case, one cannot be said
to *know* what is not the case. These are the considerations
by reference to which knowledge, when contrasted with
falsity or error, is always correct or true.

What truth may be supposed to be is indeed a troublesome question. However, it can be said with reasonable
accuracy that when truth is considered to be a matter of
the truth of knowledge-claims to the effect that such and
such is so, and when these claims are empirical, by which
is meant capable of being denied without self-contradic-
tion, truth is generally held to consist in some sort of correspondence—correspondence between the knowledge-
claim and what, in some sense or other, is the case. This
view is commonly referred to as "the correspondence
theory of truth."

The correspondence theory of truth is not without difficulties, but it is none the less widely endorsed even by
those cognizant of its difficulties. The recognition that
knowledge-claims may depend for their meaning on con-
ceptual context and that it would be naive to suppose
that true assertions are in some simple way "pictures of
facts" is not sufficient to undermine the theory. What we
seek is some sort of functional congruence between assertions or knowledge-claims and natural happenings or with
what we may call, in some broad sense, actuality. The
chief rival of the correspondence theory of truth is the coherence theory of truth, and it must be admitted that this
latter has an intellectual appeal in that it avoids the troublesome problem of just how we are to construe the relationship of correspondence. Even so, it is not to be expected that the correspondence theory of truth will be
easily relinquished. The great enterprise of acquiring
knowledge, in the sense of knowledge about, and this

not only in science but in common affairs, seems to lose its savor, its force, its vitality, without the assumption of something to which it is in some way answerable. Also, however much we may dismiss this theory as "impenetrably obscure" we have a way of reverting to it. When, as philosophers, we brood on the difficulty of finding an acceptable account of just what this independent matter-of-fact or state-of-affairs, this recalcitrant something, might be supposed to be, we may be strongly tempted to abandon the notion entirely, but when, as active agents grappling with events, we face decision and have to stake success or possibly more *on* decision, the sense of that obdurate something floods back upon us with full force. Now we voice the urgent question: But what, as a matter of actual fact, *is* the case? We do this, however much, in some earlier moment of detached reflection, we may have looked with favor on some philosophic suggestion which was designed to rid us of the obscure notion of truth as a matter of correspondence.

But it is one thing to endorse, whatever its difficulties, some version of the correspondence theory of truth, and another thing to say that *any* use of the word "knowledge" is logically tied to this notion of truth, or, for the matter of that, to any notion of truth. Of course, when "knowledge" is contrasted with "error," knowledge just *is* truth, but we cannot confine the use of the word "knowledge" exclusively to this context. We are not always engaged in asserting that such and such is so; we are often engaged in the activity of "entertaining" in the sense of reflecting on something. To be sure, if we should choose to insist that this is always and necessarily a matter of logical reasoning we can introduce the notion of truth as logical cogency, but it is simply not plausible to suppose that every case of entertainment, motivated by the desire for improved understanding, is a case of logical reasoning. To understand, in the sense of "enter into" and "seek to realize," is not the same as to carry out some process of inference.

Still, it is necessary to be more precise with respect to just what is involved in "seeking to realize." This *could* be interpreted as seeking to understand the relationship of part to part in some complex structure. For example, I may seek to realize the complex pattern of a musical composition or the complex pattern of a work of architectural art. It is sensible to say that in doing this I am seeking to know it better, and the question: How well do you know it? is perfectly intelligible. In the same way I may seek to realize the part-to-part relationship in a poem or other work of literary art. In addition to this, it will be noncontroversially recognized that there can be knowledge-claims about a work of art, whether literary or otherwise, and that the question of the justification of such claims can always be raised. But there remains a difference between what *we* say about a poem and what a poem says. It is because works of literature seem to "speak" that the issue of truth is more likely to be raised in reference to literature than in reference to other arts. I am not, of course, claiming that all critics and artists raise this issue, but it is the case that reference to truth is more likely to be encountered in literary than in other criticism and that literary artists are more likely to talk about the struggle for truth than nonliterary artists. Assuming that the tendency to this talk is something that must be accounted for, we shall have to consider what "truth" in such a connection might mean.

Taking for granted, as I now must, that the kind of knowledge literature can afford is understanding as realization in the particular sense of the realization of what something might come to as a form of lived experience, we can recognize that literature is not adequately thought of as direct report about something and that if there *is* a meaning of "truth" that is relevant to literature it must be different from the meaning of "truth" as associated with specifically formulated knowledge-claims about this or that. Is there a meaning of "truth" that is distinguishably different? There is; this is truth in the sense of authenticity.

The meaning of "true" as authentic or genuine is perfectly familiar and established in our language. Also, it has a counterpart in the false as the fake and the spurious. These meanings are so familiar that no one is likely to question them. However, it might be quickly said that *these* meanings of "true" and "false" are obviously noncognitive, they can have no relation to anything we might call knowledge. A relationship to knowledge comes in only when we have a claim that something is genuine or that something is spurious; and such claims, like other knowledge-claims, can be true or false, but then in the sense of correct or incorrect. I shall undertake to argue that this quick disposal of the issue is altogether too hasty.

I certainly have no wish to blur these differences in meaning of "true" and "false"; being authentic is not the same thing as being correct, and the judgment that something is fake, bogus and spurious has a far stronger normative force than attaches to the judgment that something is incorrect. Thus, though I propose to argue that "authentic" and "inauthentic" have some relation to knowledge, when knowledge is understood in a particular way, I do not wish to suggest that this is the same as the relation associated with "correct" and "incorrect."

To discern what is here involved we have to go back to the notion of understanding as realization and back, beyond that, to the notion of "an experience." I do not propose to rehearse arguments already presented—I shall have to assume the cogency of these arguments—but it will be necessary to talk again about "an experience" and the kind of understanding it might afford. Let us put aside, for the moment, the more complicated issue of literary art and consider "an experience" as life experience.

Every case of an experience, in the singular sense, involves a duality between the self who undergoes the experience and the self who is aware of the manner in which the experiencing self experiences. Now, when an experience is life experience and is my experience, I must be acknowledged to be a privileged observer, and there is something impertinent in your undertaking to tell me what and how I experience. Still, the very involvement that makes me a privileged observer can make me a prejudiced observer as could happen when conventional assumptions about what ought to be experienced in certain situations are semi-consciously operative. This "ought" can be a matter of what is proper in the sense of permissible, or of what is proper in the sense of "to be expected."

At first glance it might seem that if prejudice operates in my apprehension of my experience, it operates in just the same way as in cases of inquiry, that is, in cases of knowledge about something. But reflection suggests that there is a difference. In cases of inquiry prejudice operates to falsify judgment, but having or undergoing an experience is not a matter of judgment. In the case of lived experience, prejudice can operate to modify the character of the experience.

Stereotyped, conventional assumptions about what is to be experienced and how it is to be experienced can, in some measure at least, make the experience stereotyped and conventional. Because of this operative influence there is a sense in which error is impossible, but yet there is a kind of falsification in that the experience is not what it might have been if it had been encountered and undergone with freedom and freshness, with unprejudiced candor and honesty. To be sure, the experience is what it is, but *as* it is, it is to some extent factitious, contrived and faked. To say that it has been forced into some conventional pattern is not to deny that, as so forced, it has this pattern, but it is to say that, for this very reason, it is deficient in genuineness and authenticity. Inauthenticity in experience is what some existentialists refer to as "mauvaise foi"; it can be considered a kind of self-deception. Does self-deception deceive? Certainly. How much is, of course, another matter. Deep self-deception may be such that the individual is unable to detect it, but partial self-deception is a common state of affairs. If we keep in mind the complicated "I-and-myself" involvement characteristic of "an experience," it will not be difficult to recognize the possibility of protective self-deceptions that are practised because they work to some extent but work uneasily. The self is to some degree aware of the dishonesty it practises on itself. We can catch ourselves insisting to ourselves that the experience is thus and so, but the vehemence of our insistence is the sign that somehow we know otherwise. Authenticity in actual experience depends on a certain kind of spiritual freedom. This freedom can be something hard won by deliberate discipline, but it can also be the unsolicited gift of temperament or of happy circumstances. We have all encountered free spirits who seem to be naturally free. To say this is no more than to acknowledge the hard fact that what some of us must win, others just have. Against the background of the recognition that experience, as life experience, can be more or less authentic and genuine, or more or less contrived and faked, we can turn to the consideration of literary art.

If it be correct to say that literature is concerned with human experience, if its enterprise is to transform whatever it uses into the substance of virtual experience, if it is primarily through literary art that we can most adequately understand what anything might come to as a form or mode of lived experience, then it is appropriate to suppose that at least part of the talent of the talented literary

artist is his greater perceptiveness with regard to the possibilities of experience. This greater perceptiveness is not
the same thing as systematic inquiry. We can have systematic inquiry into human experience as into anything,
else, but this is something quite different. Systematic inquiry depends on the outside view and its product is
knowledge about. But knowledge as realization depends
on the inside view, on what is to be discerned by imaginative participation. The talented literary artist is commonly
far more adventurous with regard to the possibilities of
experience than the ordinary person, and it is particularly
true of him that "nothing human is totally alien." This
may account for T. S. Eliot's statement that literary creation is not the expression of personality but the escape
from personality, and for Keats's statement in a letter to
Richard Woodhouse: "The poet is the most unpoetical
of any thing in existence, because he has no Identity—he
is continually in for and filling some other Body—The
Sun, the Moon, the Sea and Men and Women, who are
creatures of impulse, are poetical, and have about them an
unchangeable attribute; the poet has none, no identity—
he is certainly the most unpoetical of all God's Creatures."

This seems, but I think only seems, to be in contradic-
tion to something we, as readers, are aware of and that is,
also of importance with reference to literary art, namely,
the sense of "literary personality" the sense of "voice."
Literature is not only linguistic, it somehow *speaks*. We
have a direct sense of distinctively human utterance, of
"man speaking" and speaking in some characteristic tone
of voice. Even the annonymous poem speaks. It is this that
accounts for the view that literary expression is somehow
personal in contrast to the impersonality of theoretical
discourse. It is this that accounts for the interest, often carried to extravagant length, in the person of the literary artist and in the facts of his biography. We all know that this
interest can be pursued in a way that is totally irrelevant

to the better understanding of literature, but the fact that it tends to be more pronounced in literary criticism than in musical, architectural, or other art criticism, cannot be explained by the simple remark: "Oh well, many literary critics are inveterate gossips." There is something about literary art that makes it different not only from other writing but also from other art. What I am suggesting here is that the sense of literary personality is something more than the sense of distinctive or characteristic art style. We are aware of Mozartean style, and we know, of course, that Mozart was a person, but we could, I think, entertain in imagination the contrary-to-fact supposition that Mozart was an angel or that this music that we hear is "the music of the spheres." We could never suppose that any work of literary art, even the poem that is predominantly melodic, "a verbal earthly paradise," is anything other than something *distinctively human* in origin and utterance. This is not just because it is linguistic. The enterprise of imagining that Copernicus's *Revolution of the Heavenly Spheres* is something composed by an intelligent but nonhuman being is difficult but yet not impossible. It is because what literary art presents, it presents as a form of virtual experience, and because, despite the important difference between virtual and actual experience, we already have some understanding of what authenticity and inauthenticity mean as regards our own actual experience, that we find it possible and even natural to speak of authenticity and inauthenticity with reference to literature.

Authenticity in life experience would seem to be partly a matter of perceptive ability and partly a matter of candor and sincerity. The idea that sincerity may have something to do with literary art has often been suggested, but it needs to be considered rather carefully. Perhaps the first thing to notice here is that artistic sincerity is not just sincerity. The literary artist is, of course, both person and artist; and though it would be incorrect to say that what he is as person has nothing to do with what he is as artist, it is still appropriate to recognize that literary creation is a special activity and that, as such, it can be associated with the assumption or acceptance of special obligations. The primary obligation of any artist, in his role as artist, is to his yet uncreated or partly created work of art, but literary art being what it is, the acceptance of obligation involves some process of suffering in the sense of undergoing. However, since artistic sincerity is a matter of enactment or evasion, it is best understood by the artist himself. The external observer, as reader or critic, can judge the art work, the product of artistic creation, but if artistic sincerity is a matter of what goes on in the making, the artist is in a better position to apprehend what it is. Certainly it is only the artist who can directly experience temptations to evasion of obligation. For example, it is only the artist who can hear the voice of the tempter who says: "After all, you have at your command some considerable technical competence. You don't need to commit yourself so thoroughly. You are surely, by now, skillful enough to do it off the top of your head." The artist, like the rest of us, can be assailed by the distractions of pain, anxiety, and fatigue, and although art is something that elicits dedication more easily than many other enterprises, there is always the possibility of the intrusion of clamorous desires for things other than good poems.

The question of sincerity is sometimes swept aside by critical theorists as utterly irrelevant, and this position is usually supported by such rhetorical questions as: "Is it not manifestly the case that the most artistically deplorable poems can be written by the most sincere persons?" But if "sincere," as it functions in this context, is intended to refer to sincere belief in some doctrine, sentiment, or idea expressed in the poem, this question misses the point. It is indeed the case that the sincere religious believer, sincere patriot, social reformer, or whatever, can be guilty of composing verse that is artistically deplorable, but though what an artist believes is not irrelevant to what he creates, it is surely a mistake to equate artistic sincerity with mere sincerity of belief. In point of fact, intense ardor of belief, unassociated with comparable or more intense ardor for art, can be a source of artistic insincerity. Passionate conviction concerning the correctness and the importance of some doctrine may be just the thing to suggest to the writer that it does not particularly matter how it is articulated provided "the message" is clear. In short, if one is possessed of the truth, in the sense of the truth about something, it may appear unnecessary to undergo the creative ordeal of making it true in the sense of authentic.

However, if artistic sincerity is a matter of enactment or evasion, a matter of what goes on in the making, sincerity is a term that more properly qualifies persons than poems. It is natural enough for the artist to suppose that the created art work will bear the outward and visible sign of the inward and spiritual grace of artistic sincerity, and, of course, there is some justification in this belief, for it would be highly implausible to suppose that there is no connection whatever between the effort of the artist and the character of the work. Nevertheless, because of the enormously important and variable factor of talent, the connection is not such as to allow us to regard as just two sides of the same coin sincerity in the artist and authenticity in the poem. As readers and critics what we must be concerned with is authenticity as characterizing poems and other works of literary art.

Since "true," whatever meaning we ascribe to it, is one of those words that needs an opposite, for without this shadow it loses its substance, it is sometimes suggested that truth can have no relevance to literature on the ground that it would be odd to speak of a false work of literature. But why should it be thought odd? The true as the authentic has its counterpart in the false as the inauthentic, and it makes, I believe, intelligible sense to speak of inauthenticity in literary expression. Let us consider what this might be. The two most obvious cases would be the pretentious and the banal.

In the case of the pretentious we have the impression of some imposing façade with nothing or next to nothing behind it. This could be just obviously inflated rhetoric—language on the loose. This gives the impression of inauthenticity because language on the loose is language not earned. But we may also arrive at an impression of inauthenticity when we have first been impressed and then disillusioned. The language of the poem gives intimations of high obliquity, suggesting the presence of elaborate depth meaning, but when we seek to penetrate to this we find no passage. Surface statement is not only the locus of the artist's control; it is for the reader the portal of entrance into the poem. There can be no entrance into the poem if surface meaning does not, in fact, exercise any control over implicit meaning. If we conclude that no such control operates we shall have the impression of something faked. Of course the failure can be the failure of the reader. No one doubts this. My intent here is merely to defend the intelligibility, not necessarily the justification, of the condemnation: "false, fake, bogus."

In the case of the banal the impression of inauthenticity is produced by the sense of borrowed language. The voice that speaks is not *a* voice, it has no distinctive note, it could be anyone's voice. We are reminded of what goes on in life when persons seek to protect themselves from the impact of experience by "forms of words." Some linguistic utterance, safely commonplace, and preferably edifying, can be quickly interposed as a protective shield. What we think of this in life will depend a good deal on what the occasion is. The stereotyped language of politeness can be justified on several grounds. It is when we suspect that "forms of words" are operative either for self-deception or for disengagement when the situation makes this inadmissible that we raise a question. But however much our awareness of the exigencies of life may be productive of tolerance, it is still the case that all stereotyped language, just because it is anyone's language, is not any individual speaker's language. The banal and the trite in literary expression can be simply failure of talent but this makes no difference, it is still inauthentic. The sense of borrowed language infects the whole presentation so that it will seem to be something taken over at second hand and therefore not genuine.

There are further, though perhaps less obvious cases of the inauthentic. These are the cases where we have the impression of "the will attempting to do the work of the imagination." We can speak of the formal intention of a novel, meaning by this that the greater part of the work is such as to provide a strong intimation of what is the case in this imaginative world, for example, that certain fictional characters are intended to have and to retain certain moral attributes, but this is counteracted by what appears to be some forced development. It is as if the author, though unable "to make it so," is, nevertheless, determined "to have it so." Something more than mere inconsistency is here involved, for we complain of falsification and contrivance.

Still another case is the intrusion of the author—not just intrusion, intrusion in a particular way. We may now prefer not to be suddenly addressed as "dear reader," but we can recognize that such address was, after all, part of an earlier literary convention. A kind of intrusion that makes for an impression of inauthenticity is the argumentative intrusion. We are not "shown," we are "told." Insistent argumentative telling will appear, in the context of literary art, as insecure protest. This is because, however much argument is perfectly acceptable in discursive writing, in the context of literary art it will appear as a substitute for the kind of persuasiveness we expect. We are reminded of what goes on in life when vehement insistence that "It *is!* It *is!*" betrays only too evidently nervous protest born of lack of assurance. In life we ask: "What is he trying to pretend to himself that he has to protest so much?" To be sure, the abandonment, on the part of the literary artist, of his enterprise of imaginative enstatement and his reversion to direct preaching of doctrine may be simply another case of failure of talent; all the same the work of literature will produce the impression of inauthenticity. Perhaps there are additional cases of intrusion—cases where we have a sense of the author drawing attention to himself, posturing about in the work of literature and saying, in effect: "See what a bold man am I!"

Since authenticity in literary art might be described as power of imaginative enstatement, the question can be raised: Does this mean anything more than simply some pervasive quality of liveliness, of animation? I believe that it does. There are two meanings that can be ascribed to the word "life." "Life," as contrasted with "death," can mean animation, vitality, but "life" means something different when it refers to life experience. It is a common assumption that all art, when successful, has a semblance of life in the sense of a kind of vitality. The judgment: "It is dead, inert, lifeless" is taken as adverse comment. Animation in this sense is not secured by mere sensuous assault. We all know that a musical presentation that abounds in clamor, or a pictorial presentation that cries aloud in color dissonance and slash, may, nevertheless, be dead, and that something that is, by contrast, delicate, may live with enduring life. There is, of course, no formula for constructing an art work that will have this semblance of life, but we can recognize, after the event, the fact of this mysterious achievement. What we can say of all art we can say of literary art, but literary art has characteristics of

its own. Truth, as authenticity, is not to be simply identified with animation, even if animation in literary art is
dependent on truth as authenticity.

All art can provide us with experience in the obvious
sense of providing something *to be* experienced, but literary art provides us with experience of experience, and
this is different. I do not wish to insist that nothing of this
sort is ever in the least characteristic of nonliterary art. For
example, pictorial art, having not only depiction but em-
ploying depiction for the presentation of what we may
call "portrayal theme," can, through the manner of depiction, provide an interpretation of portrayal theme, and
this has some similarity to the enterprise of literature.
Most portrayal themes are, in fact, derived from literary
sources; in western art these sources are predominantly
biblical and classical—Abraham about to sacrifice Isaac,
or Bacchus appearing to Ariadne on the island of Naxos.
In such cases pictorial art can be said to have a certain affinity with literature. Still, no lover of pictorial art will be
likely to say that a pictorial artist neglects portrayal theme
at his peril; *Still Life with Lemons* is perfectly acceptable
if well composed, and, indeed, in some quarters, more
acceptable. It is also, no doubt, the case that we sometimes
hear the condemnation "fake, bogus, spurious!" with
reference to nonliterary art, and intended with a meaning
other than the meaning involved in "faked Vermeer,"
but it surely is evident that reference to authenticity, or
the lack of it, is far more frequent in literary comment.
All this is understandable if we recognize the deep involvement of literary art with experience as lived experience,
and if we recognize that we understand the kind of thing
realization and authenticity are as an achievement, or partial achievement, in life experience. For any judgment of
authenticity in reference to a work of literature we draw,
of course, on our funded knowledge of other works of literature, but we also draw on our experience of life. When

we pronounce something to be authentic or inauthentic we are not saying that it corresponds or fails to correspond to some sort of knowledge about this or that, neither are we checking it for some sort of plausibility; we are saying, in effect, "It rings true" or "It rings false." This has a perfectly intelligible meaning. If anyone proposes to question its meaning let us ask him: "How is it in life experience? Is it possible for life experience, as an experience, to be genuine and authentic or, on the contrary, falsified, faked, and contrived?" If this question is not understood, our only recourse will be to direct the obstinate nonunderstander *to* works of literature, for authentic works of literary art can display, as part of their total presentational meaning, the spectacle of fictional characters busily engaged in this very activity of falsifying and faking their experience.

IX

Concluding Remarks

WHAT is the cause of the sea storm? It is the anger of the god Poseidon. How wrong this is, but yet, how understandable! It is wrong as an answer to the question asked, and wrong in a radically uncorrectable way. We know this now. Animistic explanation of natural phenomena, the extension to nature at large of the kind of purposive causality man is familiar with in the case of his own actions, will not work. Yet it is an easily understood mode of explanation, for if one *were* a sea god and *were* angry one would create precisely this turbulence. The immediate intelligibility of the explanation counts for it, and makes it resistant to falsification. Nor need we wonder why the recognition of the inadequacy of the explanation was delayed. The action prompted by the explanation is some ceremony of propitiation: make sacrifice of appropriate animals or cast treasure into the depths. This ceremony will not work but, given the kind of explanation, nonefficacy in particular cases can always be explained. The sacrifice was inadequate, the ritual was wrongly performed, the anger was too great, and, as final resort, who can read the mind of a god? But there is more to it than this. The animistic view is appropriate to the human experience of undergoing a sea storm.

We can bring this out by changing the question from:

What is the cause of the sea storm? to: What might the human experience of undergoing a sea storm be like? Now we speak most aptly when we say: "The sea is angry." Anger, threat, menace are apprehended as phenomenally objective, "out there" in the sea. The struggle of the mariner with the storm is experienced as combat. The force opposing him is felt as similar in kind to the force with which he battles it. The ship itself is now a live thing that leaps and shudders and labors in the waves. Now we feel the power of the god, and this is why Poseidon is still relevant even in an age of science.

Although it is a matter of historical record that literary artists and lovers of literature have, from time to time, nourished and voiced resentment against natural science, seen as "the destroyer of rainbows," yet it appears by now to be generally recognized that the scientific and the literary approach to natural phenomena cannot possibly be rivals. Rivals must do battle on common ground and there is here too little common ground for genuine contention. The poem that tells us that the moon is a goddess, or love-sick, or lunatic, is as intelligible and valid as it ever was. Natural science cannot be of direct help or hindrance to the literary artist although, of course, the artist who happens to take an interest in it may derive from that interest the stimulus of new perspectives, above all, perhaps, material for metaphor. Lunar landscape, understood in terms of contemporary astronomical theory, may well provide the raw material out of which reanimated metaphor might be forged. The literary importance will, of course, reside in the reanimation, not in the fact that what has been used for this purpose is something more scientifically "up to date." Any branch of natural science, biology, crystallography, or whatever, may stir the imagination of the literary artist, and anything that stirs his imagination is potential raw material for artistic exploitation. "Raw material" and "exploitation" are the operative

words. If you wish to receive the best account to date of
the structure and operation of natural phenomena, you
must turn to the scientist. It is useless to expect that the
literary artist will submit himself to the discipline necessary for science. As private person he might do this, but as
literary artist he will not. As artist he has, of course, his
own discipline, but this is something other than the discipline of science.

The situation is not really different if the science in
question is psychology rather than, for example, as-
tronomy. It is unfortunate, because confusing, that the
word "psychology" is used with reference to both science
and literary art, but, since this is so, we shall need to distinguish scientific psychology from literary psychology.
Scientific psychology is the science of behavior; literary
psychology is the art of imagining how persons might
think, feel, and experience. Literary psychology was not,
in the past, dependent on scientific psychology, *and it is
not so dependent now.* It is one thing for a literary artist
to take an interest in psychological theory, for example,
the theories of Freud or of Jung, and exploit these as raw
material for artistic construction; it would be another, and
a foolish, thing, for any artist to suppose that this is to be
accepted as doctrine to which he must conform. What has
rendered these theories attractive to some literary artists
is their mythic mode of presentation, but it is precisely this
mode of presentation that can be expected to undergo revision into something more scientifically manageable; certainly Freud may be recognized as an important scientific
pioneer, but proper respect for pioneer thinkers has
never stood in the way of scientific revision.

The advice: "Do not go to literary art for doctrine,"
should not be interpreted to mean that literature cannot
deal with ideas. As we know, the most elaborate ideational material can find accommodation in literary art,
and its presence there need not be supposed to render the

work of literature "impure." What makes a work of literature impure is the lumpish presence of unassimilated, untransformed, raw material. Doctrine, simply as such, is, from the literary point of view, no more than raw material, because what is important in literature is the revelation of the humanistic import of doctrine. I do not wish to deny that there is a sense in which doctrine "comes alive" in impressive works of literary art, for imaginative participation in belief provides an illumination not otherwise to be had. Let us recognize the ambiguity of the term "implication." If we speak of the implications of some doctrine, we might mean what it presupposes and what may be inferred from it, but we might also mean what it comes to as something not only thought, but felt, lived, experienced. Knowing by vicarious living through is not the same as knowing about; each mode of knowing provides its own illumination, and neither is an adequate substitute for the other.

Although by now it is supposed to be a critical commonplace that form and content in literary art are intimately related, in that, though either can be independently talked about, neither can be independently appraised, yet there remains, in some quarters, a certain hankering for independent appraisal of content. Let us consider, in this connection, the frequently quoted remark of T. S. Eliot: "The greatness of literature cannot be determined solely by literary standards; but we must remember that whether it is literature or not can be determined only by literary standards." Since Eliot has said other things that are theoretically incompatible with this, it will be appropriate to consider the view here expressed independently of authorship. There are many puzzling things about this view, not the least of which is that anyone inclined to reject the claim will be accused of entertaining narrow notions of literary art as mere eloquence of discourse, yet it could be argued that it is precisely this narrow notion to which the defenders of the view are committed. This is because if greatness in literature is to be appraised by trans-literary judgment, it follows that what makes literature literature must be exclusively a matter of eloquent advocacy. There is here some logical confusion over the use of the word "literature" in that the advocates of this view seem to wish to say: Literature to be great must be more than literature, but the view of literature as more than literature is the right view of literature. Nevertheless, those who voice this opinion are attempting to accommodate something which must be seriously considered.

The wish to distinguish between goodness and greatness in literary achievement is natural enough. With regard to literary art, as with regard to all art, we can recognize a difference between relatively modest and relatively ambitious undertakings. The relatively modest enterprise may show forth as fully successful, we may be moved to pronounce it perfect, and feel no inclination to wish that it were in any way different. Yet success, even somewhat flawed success, in highly ambitious undertaking is bound to strike us as impressive, and this is not only natural but entirely appropriate. However, this distinction is one that can be made with reference to any art: the successful dance melody is not the elaborate symphonic composition, and the delightful garden pavilion is not the great cathedral. But judgment of greatness in these cases would be musical or architectural and so the question arises: What is there about literature that might suggest the view that greatness in literature "cannot be determined solely by literary standards"?

There are at least two characteristics of literary art that might prompt this view. In the first place, a work of literature presents us not simply with something to be experienced but with experience to be experienced. In the second place, literary art abounds in the expression of what may be called valuational attitudes, that is to say, attitudes "pro" or "con," attitudes of endorsement or rejection. The expression of valuational attitudes is usually indirect in literature but all the more effective for this indirection. The persuasive character which literary art has in this respect has often been acknowledged, somewhat ruefully, by philosophers. If the philosopher, as moralist, should speak up and say that X is good and Y is bad, voices are raised on all sides to demand that he produce supporting reasons to back this claim, but the literary artist does not need to voice any direct claim, for he can create an imaginative world in which X shows forth as bright, luminous, and desirable, and Y shows forth as shadowed, as suspicious, as undesirable. The moralist must voice a claim, but the artist can evoke the imaginative experience of apprehending things in a certain valuational perspective.

Now since what literary art presents is not simply something to be experienced, but experience to be experienced, we can appropriately raise the question of the range or depth of the virtual experience expressed or embodied in the work of literature. This carries us beyond such purely formal considerations as unity in variety or complexity with order, and if this is what is meant by saying that a purely formalistic approach, such as may be adequate for other art, will not be satisfactory for literary art, the claim, I believe, is cogent. But if greatness in literary art should be a matter of magnitude, of range or depth of virtual experience, is there any sufficient reason to suppose that the judgment about this is something other than a literary judgment? To say that it is a literary judgment is to concede that it is entirely a matter of treatment and that, I think, is what must be conceded. The argument for this consists in exhibiting the embarrassments attendant on the alternative position.

Those who advocate the appropriateness of a trans-literary judgment have too much literary tact and sensibility to wish to endorse the view that "right opinions," "edifying sentiments," "proper valuations" will of themselves suffice to confer literary salvation. This is why it is specified that candidates for trans-literary judgment must already have passed the test of literary salvation. Now it seems, but I think it only seems, that once you can assume literary salvation, as a matter of treatment, you can single out for separate appraisal *what* has been so treated. But the troublesome question arises: How do we discern the object of this evaluative judgment? The only way we can do this is to abstract it by giving independent expression to the "point of view," "valuational assumptions," "set of beliefs" operative in the work of literature, and this returns us to the unhappy situation of being called upon to judge the rightness of views, simply as such, and independently of how they function in the context of the literary structure.

The crucial question is the question: What is of primary importance in literary art; is it doctrine or is it experience? This question must be asked because there is a difference between the enterprise of debating doctrine, and the enterprise of appraising the range and depth of virtual experience. The assertion that in literary art treatment is everything will, of course, be likely to be resisted if this is interpreted to mean "rhetoric is everything" or "it does not matter what the poet says but only how he says it," but the view that treatment is everything should, I think, be interpreted to mean that just as no summary statement of plot, so no mere statement of valuational assumptions can tell us about the merit of a work of literature.

If we should undertake the intellectual enterprise of eliciting the set of valuational assumptions operative in a certain kind of contemporary subliterature, we may be tempted to suppose that the subliterary status of these stories is an inevitable consequence of the nature of the assumptions. Consider the following summary statement of assumptions: "Nothing unfortunate can really happen to a truly kind and good person. The best things are the things that are readily available to everyone. All things excellent are as easy as they are common. Traditional modes of thought and action are sound, so that anyone who supposes he knows better than grandmother is wrong and will be unhappy. Such an unhappy mistaken person can, however, be saved by the sudden recognition of the deep wisdom couched in the homely remark of some aged peripheral character who has never left his native corner and who is, as nearly as possible, illiterate." When we consider such simplistic assumptions as these we may be tempted to suppose that nothing *can* be made of them, but surely the more judicious conclusion is that, in sub-literary composition, nothing *is* made of them, and for the reason that they are used again and again merely as formula for story construction.

If we take account of the diversity of impressive works of literary art we cannot suppose that there is some particular state-of-affairs that is *the* human condition, and that it is the task of literary artists to be correct about it. The reader of literature may very well find certain valuational perspectives congenial to his temperament, or more directly relevant to his social and historical situation. Personal preference, on such a basis, is natural and it would be foolish to quarrel with it. All the same, the reader of literature who aspires to possess himself of his literary inheritance cannot afford to listen only to those voices that seem to speak directly to his situation. Literary education can enormously expand the range of humanistic understanding, but this is not the same as "solving problems" or "providing answers." He who must have answers, and quickly, will be better advised to look elsewhere for them. The realm of literary art is a realm too diverse, too various, too rich in multiple perspectives, to provide anything in the way of simple directives.

No theoretical discourse can be expected to have the extraordinary toughness, the extraordinary survival power, of successful literary art. This is not because literary artists "write better"; it is because they write differently. This survival power is, of course, a function of the high degree of autonomy and self-sufficiency characteristic of literary structure, but agreement on this matter by no means insures agreement on why it is so. One view, of course, is that literary art survives because, or in so far as, it wisely renounces all commerce with that perishable commodity known as knowledge. Knowledge is always undergoing revision, modification, reformulation. Literary art survives because as free creation, free invention, it is, or aspires to be, simply and solely an aesthetically alluring beautiful structure. Now, in so far as this view is the product of dissatisfaction with certain theories about literature as cognitively significant, theories which regard works of literature as vehicles of doctrine, or theories which regard them as illustrative, "just representations of general human nature," it is not difficult to understand why the purely formalistic view might be resorted to as a device for disallowing such assumptions. One can sympathize with this. However, in so far as this view is prompted by the desire for some sort of aesthetic purity, it is based, I think, on the wrong notion of purity, and in so far as it is prompted by the desire to see literary art as aspiring to the condition of some other art, "aspiring to the condition of music," for example, it is a view that will fail to do justice to the distinctive potentialities of literary art.

There is, I believe, another, and more plausible, explanation of the tough survival power of successful literary art. Such literary art survives because it transforms whatever material it deals with into the substance of lived experience. This virtual experience is available for imaginative apprehension by the reader because the literary artist has "done the work" of rendering it available. This does not mean that it is always easily available but only that it is available. It is available because it has been shaped, formed, and structured in such a way that the literary presentation can exercise control over the experience of the reader. I am here, of course, presupposing a good reader: a reader prepared to submit himself to the control exercised by the work of literature.

Is one claiming too much in speaking of such control? Is one assuming too much in saying that virtual experience as embodied, incarnated, in literary art is shareable in a sense in which actual experience never can be? Supposing it be said: "We cannot hope to understand the literary art of another age or culture because this literature is based on beliefs, attitudes, the climate of opinion, the spiritual outlook, of an alien character." The question arises: How do we discern that this is the case? Is it from nonliterary sources that we arrive at this discernment or is it the works of literature themselves that tell us? It must be the latter, for the only evidence that there is an alien element would be the finding of such an element. Now, to be sure, if this finding is the finding of the incomprehensible, if encounter with the work of literature produces bafflement, then indeed we can conclude that we do not understand, but would we, in such a case, go on to speak of "spiritual outlook," "distinctive attitude," "mode of vision"? I think not. Any such talk presupposes a good deal of understanding. Surely there would be something odd about the suggestion: "Enter imaginatively into the virtual experience embodied in this work of literary art and you will recognize how incomprehensibly alien it is." Any sense of the alien would have to be based on the awareness of difference between this and that "point of view," "mode of vision," both of which have been vicariously experienced. But what has been vicariously experienced is no longer fully alien. The claim that we cannot in imagination transcend the peculiarities of our age, our culture, our situation, might be dogmatically asserted on the rather ill-defined ground that "it just stands to reason," but argument in defense of it is likely to be circular argument. This will be the case if the "alien otherness" we cite as evidence for the impossibility of participation has been derived from an understanding of works of literature we claim to be inaccessible. If anyone wants to point out that we cannot actually be Athenians of the fifth century, contemporaries of Donne or of Fielding, the fact can be freely admitted. If anyone wants to say that the perspective on a work of literature is modified, not only by the general ongoing process of history, but also by the development of the strictly literary tradition, this too can be acknowledged. Nevertheless, if the kind of understanding we seek is understanding as realization through participation in shared experience, the sensible question can and should be asked: If successful literary art is not fully satisfactory, what would be better? To fail to prize the best that is available on the ground that it falls short of some admittedly unattainable ideal must surely be misguided.

It will now, I hope, be possible to sum up. This essay does not attempt to offer a comprehensive theory of literature. It has been concerned with a single question: What kind of knowledge, if any, does literary art afford? The answer I propose is that literary art, when functioning successfully as literary art, provides knowledge in the form of realization: the realization of what anything might come to as a form of lived experience. The kind of knowledge, as well as the manner of knowing, is something familiar to us on the basis of life experience, and it receives acknowledgment in the common remark: "You don't really know what it is unless and until you've experienced it." This is knowing by living through, and it is something distinguishably different from knowing about.

All knowing involves duality; there is no good reason for calling mere awareness knowledge. Nevertheless, it is a mistake to suppose that the only passage from mere awareness to knowledge is by the path of inference, so that anything properly describable as knowledge must be inferential knowledge about something. I have sought to argue, as cogently as I can, that the essential difference between what is just experience and what is *an* experience is that *an* experience involves duality. *An* experience, as actual experience, is self-consciously recognized by the experiencer as his. This involves a duality of the self: the I-me duality. Thus *an* experience involves the apprehension of what is experienced, together with the apprehension of the manner in which what is experienced is experienced. The importance of literary art, from the strictly cognitive point of view, is that it provides an enormous extension and elaboration of this kind of knowledge. Successful literary art is so much more ambitious and luminous than anything life affords that we may be tempted to overlook its humble analogue in common events. This overlooking is somewhat similar to the way in which, dazzled by the intellectual achievements of developed scientific knowledge, we overlook its humble analogue in simple commonsense knowledge about natural phenomena.

Everything describable as knowledge is shaped and structured in some fashion, and the more ambitious the cognitive enterprise the more elaborate the structuring is likely to be. We can be impatient with this, and there is much in the record of intellectual history that testifies to such impatience. The philosopher who tells us that propositions are pictures of facts, or that bedrock knowledge consists in the direct awareness of sense data; the historian who proposes the programme of eschewing all interpre-

tation in favor of direct report on how things actually occurred; the mystic who brushes aside all theology as necessarily misleading, exhibit a common, and quite understandable, wish for immediacy. However, nothing can be
known except as distanced, and nothing can be distanced
except as structured in some way.

There is, it might be said, a paradox about literary
art, but this is a paradox in the sense of something which,
though it may seem puzzling and odd on initial encounter,
is understandable on the basis of reflection. The kind of
knowledge and the mode of knowing afforded by successful literary art seems to have an intimacy and an immediacy not characteristic of knowledge as knowledge about
this or that. Yet this very intimacy, this very immediacy,
is a product not simply of distancing but of double distancing.

We can know *about* a work of literature as we can
know about anything else, but this knowing about has
utility as a preparation for a further and different kind of
knowing: knowing through imaginative participation. In
so far as this imaginative participation is controlled by
the literary presentation, it is a vicarious experience of a
virtual experience. How can anything so remote as this,
so twice removed, so doubly distanced seem to have about
it such an air of intimacy, of immediacy? The answer, I
think, is that what literary art presents is designed to
elicit a full response, sensuous, intellectual, and emotional, not separated but interfused. It is this fullness of
presentation and fullness of response that accounts for the
sense of immediacy. Knowing by living through is distinguishably different from knowing through the process of
inference, and the sense of its being lived experience is
associated with this, for, however much any particular
realization may involve an emphasis on the sensuous, or
the intellectual, or the emotional, this is only a matter of
emphasis. Otherwise expressed, a totality of presentation

and response is a totality regardless of how this totality is formed. But though life provides occasions for such realizations, it is to literature that we must look for the development of the implicit potentialities of this kind of knowledge. Life experience, as actual experience, is idiosyncratic, fragmentary, and fleeting; only virtual experience, structured and articulated, lifted out of the temporal flux of ongoing happening, provides something that can be fully realized and shared. Anyone who prefers communal participation in spontaneous "Happenings" to the experience of ordered art is, of course, perfectly entitled to his preference. All the same, this preference is the product of impatience. The lonely soul craves some quick alleviation of its situation, and it can, no doubt, achieve this alleviation through immersion in the Happening. Nothing is wrong with this simply as such, but it is useless to look to it for insight, illumination, revelation.

Man can be understood in many ways. Natural science will deal with him as one phenomenon among others in a natural world. History, anthropology, social and political theory, can deal with him in an intelligible and useful manner. The importance of all of this is so obvious and so universally recognized, that no one need lift his voice to point out that there *is* such a thing as inferential knowledge about man and that we stand in need of it. But literary art, as revelatory disclosure, calls for something in the nature of explanation and defense. This is not because readers and lovers of literature are likely to be startled by the claim that literary art can be revelatory. Most readers are, I think, inclined to assume that this is so, and for the very good reason that they seem to derive such revelatory insights in their commerce with works of literature. In so far as I am correct on this matter, I might be said to be preaching to the converted, but there can, after all, be a point in such preaching, since some, at least, of the converted may wish to consider a reasoned defense of the faith that is in them. In an argumentative, critical, and skeptical age a reasoned defense, if cogent, can be useful. Furthermore, I candidly confess to a certain missionary zeal in this matter. The kind of knowledge and the mode of knowing that literary art can provide seems to me so important for the quality of our human life that anything that will signal it out, emphasize it, draw attention to it, surely seems worth while. Literary art is humanistic not simply in the sense that it relates to man; it is, one might say, man's distinctive presentation of himself to himself. "Speak to me that I may see you." *This* particular speaking is the voice of literary art, and the visibility it provides is the visibility of man as total person.